The Essential Mystics

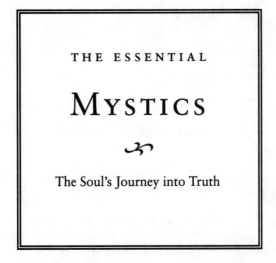

THE ESSENTIAL

MYSTICS

The Soul's Journey into Truth

Edited and with an Introduction by
Andrew Harvey

CASTLE BOOKS

MYSTICS

Published by CASTLE BOOKS
A Division of Book Sales, Inc.
114 Northfield Avenue, Edison, New Jersey 08837

ISBN 0-7858-0904-X

Manufactured in the United States of America.

For Eryk, my husband:
   "For, lo, the winter is past, the rain is over and
gone;
   The flowers appear on the earth . . . "
      Song of Songs

All paths lead to me.
   Krishna, from the Bhagavad Gita

The roads are different, the goal is one. . . . When
people come there, all quarrels or differences or
disputes that happened along the road are resolved.
Those who shouted at each other along the road "You
are wrong" or "You are an unbeliever" forget their
differences when they come there because there, all
hearts are in unison.
   Rumi

Why are we here? To become ourselves in You.
   Kabir

You must work in the world. God did not create wars.
God did not create weapons. I will give you all my help,
but your responsibility and duty are to work for a
better world.
   The Virgin to Rosa Quatrini, San Damiano, 1968

Contents

Introduction

At the beginning of his classic spiritual autobiography Bede Griffiths tells us of the mystical experience that transformed his life:

> One day during my last term at school I walked out alone in the evening and heard the birds singing in that full chorus of song, which can only be heard at that time of the year at dawn or at sunset. I remember now the shock of surprise with which the sound broke on my ears. It seemed to me that I had never heard the birds singing before and I wondered whether they sang like this all the year round and I had never noticed it. As I walked on I came upon some hawthorn trees in full bloom and again I thought I had never seen such a sight or experienced such sweetness before. If I had been brought suddenly among the trees of the Garden of Paradise and heard a choir of angels singing I could not have been more surprised. I came then to where the sun was setting over the playing fields. A lark rose suddenly from the ground beside the tree, and then sank back still singing to rest. Everything then grew still as the sunset faded and the veil of dusk began to cover the earth. I remember now the feeling of awe which came over me. I felt inclined to kneel on the ground, as though I had been standing in the presence of an angel; and I hardly dared to look on the face of the sky, because it seemed as though it was but a veil before the face of God.

Up to that time, Bede Griffiths tells us, he had lived the life of a normal schoolboy, quite content with the world as he found it. He goes on:

> I was suddenly made aware of another world of beauty and mystery such as I had never imagined to exist, except in poetry. It was as though I had begun to see and smell and hear for the first time. The world appeared to me as Wordsworth describes it with "the glory and freshness of a dream." The sight of a wild rose growing on a hedge, the scent of lime—tree blossoms caught suddenly as I rode down a hill on a bicycle, came to me like visitations from another world. But it was not only my senses that were awakened. I experienced an overwhelming emotion in the presence of

nature, especially at evening. It began to have a kind of sacramental character for me. I approached it with a sense of almost religious awe and, in a hush that comes before sunset, I felt again the presence of an almost unfathomable mystery. The song of the birds, the shape of the trees, the colors of the sunset, were so many signs of this presence, which seemed to be drawing me to itself.

Mystical experience is the direct, unmediated experience of what Bede Griffiths beautifully describes as "the presence of an almost unfathomable mystery . . . which seems to be drawing me to itself." This mystery is beyond name and beyond form; no name or form, no dogma, philosophy, or set of rituals can ever express it fully. It always transcends anything that can be said of it and remains always unstained by any of our human attempts to limit or exploit it. Every mystic of every time and tradition has awakened in wonder and rapture to the signs of this eternal Presence and known its mystery as one of relation and love, for in every tradition the Presence is represented as hungry to reveal itself and to enter into ecstatic and intimate communion with its own creation. The awe and adoration that such an experience of love brings is the hidden foundation of all authentic religion, and to deepen and re-create more and more profoundly that awe and adoration, the wisdom they awaken, and the initiation into reality that they make possible is the goal of all authentic mystical discipline. As the great Islamic mystic Rumi tells us: "Generation upon generation have passed, my friend, but these meanings are constant and everlasting. The water in the stream may have changed many times, but the reflection of the moon and the stars remains the same."

The word *mystic* may mislead or intimidate some people—the prestige accorded to it has traditionally been so exalted that they feel such heightened perception and joy belong to and are attainable by only a few chosen human beings. This is far from the case. Mystical experience is always available—like the divine grace it is—to any who really want it; and all human beings are given in the course of their lives glimpses into the heart of the real which they are free to pursue or forget. As Bede Griffiths writes of his illumination in the field at sunset:

> An experience of this kind is probably not at all uncommon, especially in early youth. Something breaks suddenly into our lives

and upsets their normal pattern and we have to begin to adjust ourselves to a new kind of existence. This experience may come, as it came to me, through nature or poetry, or through art and music; or it may come through the adventure of flying or mountaineering, or of war; or it may come simply through falling in love, or through some apparent accident, an illness, the death of a friend, a sudden loss of fortune. Anything which breaks through the routine of daily life may be the bearer of this message to the soul. But however it may be, it is as though a veil has been lifted and we see for the first time behind the facade which the world has built around us. Suddenly we know we belong to another world, that there is another dimension to existence. . . . We see our life for a moment in its true perspective in relation to eternity. We are freed from the flux of time and see something of the eternal order that underlies it. We are no longer isolated individuals in conflict with our surroundings; we are parts of a whole, elements in an universal harmony.

Mystics in all world traditions testify to what Bede Griffiths is here telling us of the scope and effect of the mystical experience. From them we come to know that what any authentic mystical opening brings us is a sense of wonder, a freedom from time's fury and anxiety, and a growing revelation of a far larger and more marvelous universe and a far vaster Identity than anything we could begin to intuit with our ordinary senses and consciousness. When we are touched by mystic grace and allow ourselves to enter its field without fear, we see that we are all parts of a whole, elements of an universal harmony, unique, essential and sacred notes in a divine music that everyone and everything is playing together with us in God and for God. And if we work patiently with what we come to know, through prayer and meditation and loving service to other beings, we will, all the traditions promise us, come to understand what Christ meant when he said, "The Kingdom of heaven is within you," and what Sultan Valad, Rumi's son, is trying to transmit to us when he writes, "A human being must be born twice. Once from his mother and again from his own body and his own existence. The body is like an egg and the essence of man must become a bird in that egg through the warmth of love, and then he must go beyond his body and fly in the eternal world of the soul."

In *The Essential Mystics* I have collected what I believe to be the most precious testimonies to this "eternal world of the soul" from all the major world traditions. I have chosen to present these testimonies not individually but grouped together in the traditions they come from, because each revelation, however personal, is always partly conditioned by the time and tradition it occurs in. Each tradition, moreover, has a different way of approaching the "unfathomable mystery," its own particular truth of insight, and represents a different way of playing the "divine music" that, Rumi says, "Love, the Supreme Musician, is always playing in our souls." Structuring the book by tradition is designed to help readers to savor in depth these different kinds of mystical music and to appreciate richly how they all echo, inspire, illumine, and complete each other.

Such an approach respects the uniqueness and integrity of each tradition while also revealing its relatedness at the deepest level to all the others. As Ramakrishna, one of humanity's greatest mystic pioneers, tells us with complete authority of experience:

I say that all are calling on the same God. . . . It is not good to feel that my religion is true and the other religions are false. All seek the same object. A mother prepares dishes to suit the stomachs of her children. Suppose a mother has five children and a fish is brought for the family. She doesn't cook the same curry for all of them. . . . God has made religions to suit different aspirants, times, and countries. All doctrines are only so many paths.

Ramakrishna speaks of God as a mother who cooks the white fish of revelation for different children in different ways; in my selection and presentation of the sacred texts in this book I have chosen to pay special attention to the sacred feminine, the motherhood of God, as understood in the different traditions. It is my belief that without the knowledge of God as Mother as well as Father and without the conscious incorporation of the healing and balancing wisdom of the sacred feminine into every part of life and every area of our understanding of the world and our relationship to it, the human race will die out and take a large part of nature with it.

Only a race in drastic denial of its interdependence with all things and beings could be devastating the environment as blindly as we are. What a recovery of the wisdom of the Mother brings to all of us is the knowledge of inseparable connection with the entire creation and the wise, active love that is born from that knowledge. Unless the human race realizes with a passion and reverence beyond thought or words its inter-being with nature, it will destroy in its greed the very environment it is itself sustained by. Unless our fundamental sacred connectedness with every being and thing is experienced deeply and enacted everywhere, religious, political, and other differences will go on creating intolerable conflict that can only increase the already dangerously high chances of our self-annihilation. The Mother's knowledge of unity, her powers of sensitivity, humility, and balance, and her infinite respect for the miracle of all life have now to be invoked by each of us and practiced if the "masculine" rational imbalance of our civilization is to be righted before it is too late.

Coming to know the hidden and forgotten Mother and the marvelous wisdom of the sacred feminine as revealed from every side and angle by the different mystical traditions is not a luxury; it is, I believe, a necessity for our survival as a species. Knowing her, we will know that we are her divine children in a relationship of complete, unconditionally loving intimacy; we will know that nature is holy in all its sacred particulars because it is everywhere vibrant with her light and her love; we will know that we have come to this earth not, as some of the patriarchal mystical traditions have implied, to escape it but to embrace it fully, not to "transcend" it but to *arrive* here in full presence, gratitude, and love.

What knowing the Mother means above all is daring to put love into action. The Mother herself is love-in-action, love acting everywhere and in everything to make creation possible. Coming into contact with the Mother is coming into contact with a force of passionate and active compassion in every area and dimension of life, a force that longs to be invoked by us to help transform all the existing conditions of life on earth so that they can mirror ever more clearly and accurately her law, her justice, and her love.

The universe, as many mystical traditions tell us, is the "child" of a sacred marriage between the feminine and masculine forces within the One, what Taoists call yin and yang, what Hindus name Shiva and Shakti; it is the constantly self-transforming expression of their eternal mutual passion. For the human race to have a chance to survive, this cosmic sacred marriage has to be mirrored and enacted in our being at every level. At every level there has to be a fusion between our masculine and feminine energies, a fusion between those polarities we have been taught to keep apart—between our vision of "heaven" and our vision of "earth," between what we have called "sacred" and what we have called "profane," between our innermost mystical awareness and our political, technological, and economic choices. Only such a fusion and "sacred marriage" can produce in us the necessary clarity, knowledge, and force of active love necessary to preserve the world. There cannot be a sacred marriage however, without a bride; until the Bride, the Mother, is recalled in all her wise splendor, the fusion of full mystical knowledge with the most committed economic and political action that alone can help us now cannot take place.

It is with the intention of helping us recall the Bride in her wise splendor that I have structured *The Essential Mystics* in the way I have. I wanted this anthology not merely to be a feast of the greatest and wisest mystical texts, but also a *practical* handbook for anyone who wants to serve as effectively as possible the new balanced humanity that is trying to be born. For this reason I have begun the anthology with the section called "Voices of the First World." In it the voices of our earliest ancestors and their Mother-wisdom are heard in all their clarity, humility, and normal visionary intimacy with nature. By placing this section first and following it with the section on Taoism—in my opinion the mystical tradition that most subtly honors the Mother and most richly embodies the sacred marriage I have been speaking of—I hope to be able to engender in readers' minds and hearts a vision of the sacred balance between the transcendent and immanent, prayer and action, body and soul that later mystical systems sometimes threatened, or even lost, in their noble but sometimes hysterical quest for transcendence. With the message of these first two sections firmly intuited, the great discoveries of the later mystical systems can be embraced and their limitations and biases toward world-denying transcendence seen and adjusted. By the end of the book I hope that readers will feel initiated into a fullness of the world's wisdom presented in a way that inspires real action in and for the world.

Teilhard de Chardin at the end of his life wrote, "Humanity is being brought to the moment when it will have to choose between suicide or adoration." We must wake up in massive numbers, and very fast, to the sacred glory of life and nature and to our sacred responsibility to preserve both or be destroyed. In this waking up the great mystics of the world are our truest and deepest and bravest friends, for together they give us the full visionary information we now need as urgently as oxygen. Armed with the highest, most balanced, and most focused insights of all the different approaches to the "almost unfathomable mystery," we still have a chance to solve our and the planet's immense problems together.

There is very little time left. Now, more than ever before, everything depends on us.

ↄ

Voices of the First World

During the last twenty years, many people have begun to realize that unless the human race listens to the "voices of the first world," the voices, that is, of those original human cultures that lived in naked and reverent intimacy with nature, it may well die out. These "voices" still speak to us in those tribal cultures that have survived against immense odds into the modern era—in, for example, the Kogi of Columbia, the Aborigines of Australia, the Hopi and Navaho of North America, the Eskimo of the Arctic Circle, and the nomads of the Himalayas.

What do these voices have to tell us? They tell us of our essential "inter-being" with nature; they tell us of the mystery of the world we inhabit, which they know to be everywhere sustained and saturated with divine presence; they tell us of the necessity of profound respect for everything that lives and happens; they tell us of a peace that is the birthright of all those who honor the Great Web of Life; they tell us of the urgency of humility before the majesty of the universe; they tell us again and again of the depth of our responsibility as human beings to be guardians of the natural world. "All life is equal," Oren Lyons, chief of the Onondaga, informed the United Nations in 1977. "We forget and we consider ourselves superior, but we are after all a mere part of the Creation. . . . We must continue to understand where we are. . . . We stand between the mountain and the ant . . . as part and parcel of the Creation. It is our responsibility, since we have been given the minds to take care of these things."

Such a radical, egalitarian vision not only reverses the arrogance of modern materialism but also implicitly challenges the world- and body-denying mysticisms and their often elitist and hierarchical modes of transmission that were to develop later. My own belief is that as consciousness of the Mother grows in our culture, we will increasingly turn to our ancestors for guidance on how to live with her and in her and for help in developing new egalitarian and "tribal" forms of transmission. We cannot go back to a tribal world, but we have many necessary lessons to learn from its "voices" and its humble practice. As is said in the Ojibway prayer quoted in this section:

Sacred One,
Teach us love, compassion, and honor
That we may heal the earth
And heal each other.

My words are tied in one
With the great mountains,
With the great rocks,
With the great trees,
In one with my body
And my heart.
Do you all help me
With supernatural power,
And you, Day,
And you, Night,
All of you see me
One with this world!
From a Yokuts prayer

THE SUPREME IO AND THE CREATION OF THE WORLD

Io dwelt within the breathing-space of immensity.
The Universe was in darkness with water everywhere.
There was no glimmer of dawn, no clearness, no light.
And he began by saying these words,—
... "Darkness become a light possessing darkness."
And at once light appeared.
(He) then repeated those self-same words in this manner . . .
"Light, become a darkness-possessing light."
And again an intense darkness supervened.
Then a third time He spake saying:
"Let there be one darkness above,
Let there be one darkness below . . .

Let there be one light above,
Let there be one light below, . . .
A dominion of light,
A bright light."
And now a great light prevailed.
(Io) then looked to the waters which compassed him about,
and spake a fourth time, saying:
"Ye waters of Tai-kama, be ye separate.
Heaven be formed." Then the sky became suspended.
"Bring forth thou Tupua-horo-nuku."
And at once the moving earth lay stretched abroad.

Those words (of Io) became impressed on the minds of our ancestors,
and by them were they transmitted down through generations, our
priest joyously referring to them as being:

The ancient and original sayings.
The ancient and original words.
The ancient and original cosmological wisdom (*wananga*).
Which caused growth from the void,
As witness the tidal waters,
The evolved heaven,
The birth-given evolved earth.
> *Maori legend*

I AM THE WIND

I am the wind that breathes upon the sea,
I am the wave on the ocean,
I am the murmur of leaves rustling,
I am the rays of the sun,
I am the beam of the moon and stars,
I am the power of trees growing,
I am the bud breaking into blossom,
I am the movement of the salmon swimming,
I am the courage of the wild boar fighting,
I am the speed of the stag running,
I am the strength of the ox pulling the plough,
I am the size of the mighty oak tree,

And I am the thoughts of all people
Who praise my beauty and grace.

From the ancient *Welsh* Black Book of Camarthan

We call upon the earth, our planet home, with its beautiful
     depths and soaring
heights, its vitality and abundance of life, and together we
     ask that it

Teach us, and show us the Way.

We call upon the mountains, the Cascades and the Olympics,
     the high green
valleys and meadows filled with wild flowers, the snows that
     never melt, the
summits of intense silence, and we ask that they

Teach us, and show us the Way.

We call upon the waters that rim the earth, horizon to hori-
     zon, that flow in our
rivers and streams, that fall upon our gardens and fields and
     we ask that they

Teach us, and show us the Way.

We call upon the land which grows our food, the nurturing
     soil, the fertile fields,
the abundant gardens and orchards, and we ask that they

Teach us, and show us the Way.

We call upon the forests, the great trees reaching strongly to
     the sky with earth in
their roots and the heavens in their branches, the fir and the
     pine and the
cedar, and we ask them to

Teach us, and show us the Way.

We call upon the creatures of the fields and forests and the
     seas, our brothers and
sisters the wolves and deer, the eagle and dove, the great
     whales and the dolphin,

the beautiful Orca and salmon who share our Northwest
    home, and we ask them to

Teach us, and show us the Way.

We call upon all those who have lived on this earth, our
    ancestors and our friends,
who dreamed the best for future generations, and upon
    whose lives our lives are
built, and with thanksgiving, we call upon them to

Teach us, and show us the Way.

And lastly, we call upon all that we hold most sacred, the
    presence and power of
the Great Spirit of love and truth which flows through all the
    Universe, to be with
us to

Teach us, and show us the Way.
                    Chinook blessing litany

THE UNIVERSAL MOTHER

The mother of our songs, the mother of all our seed, bore us in
the beginning of things and so she is the mother of all types of
men, the mother of all nations. She is the mother of the thunder, the mother of the streams, the mother of the trees and all
things. She is the mother of the world and of the older brothers,
the stonepeople. She is the mother of the fruits of the earth and
of all things. She is the mother of our youngest brothers, and
the strangers. She is the mother of our dance paraphernalia, of
all our temples and she is the only mother we possess. She
alone is the mother of the fire and the Sun and the Milky
Way. . . . She is the mother of the rain and the only mother we
possess. And she has left us a token in all temples . . . a token in
the form of songs and dances.

She has no cult, and no prayers are really directed to her, but
when the fields are sown and the priests chant their incanta-
tions the Kagaba say, "And then we think of the one and only
mother of the growing things, of the mother of all things." One

prayer was recorded. "Our mother of the growing fields, our mother of the streams, will [you] have pity upon us? For [to] whom do we belong? Whose seeds are we? To our mother alone do we belong."

Kagaba myth

O my mother Nut,
stretch your wings over me.
Let me become like the imperishable stars,
like the indefatigable stars.
May Nut extend her arms over me
and her name of
    "She who extends her arms"
    chases away the shadows
    and makes the light shine everywhere.
O Great Being who is in the world of the Dead,
At whose feet is Eternity,
In whose hand is the always,
Come to me,
O great divine beloved Soul,
who is in the mysterious abyss,
Come to me.

Ancient Egyptian prayer

Everything is laid out for you.
Your path is straight ahead of you.
Sometimes it's invisible but it's there.
You may not know where it's going,
But you have to follow that path.
It's the path to the Creator.
It's the only path there is.

Chief Leon Shenandoah

Sometimes I,
    I go about pitying
    Myself
    While I am carried by the wind
    Across the sky.

Ojibway song

SONG OF THE YOUNG WAR GOD

I have been to the end of the earth.
I have been to the end of the waters.
I have been to the end of the sky.
I have been to the end of the mountains.
I have found none that were not my friends.
Traditional Navaho song

THE EARTH IS BEAUTIFUL

The Earth is beautiful
The Earth is beautiful
The Earth is beautiful
Below the East, the Earth, its face toward the East, the top
    of its head is beautiful
Its legs, they are beautiful
Its body, it is beautiful
Its chest, it is beautiful
Its breath, it is beautiful
Its head-feather, it is beautiful
The Earth is beautiful.
Navaho song

ITS LIFE AM I

Hozhoni, hozhoni, hozhoni
Hozhoni, hozhoni, hozhoni
The Earth, its life am I, *hozhoni, hozhoni*
The Earth, its feet are my feet, *hozhoni, hozhoni*
The Earth, its legs are my legs, *hozhoni, hozhoni*
The Earth, its body is my body, *hozhoni, hozhoni*
The Earth, its thoughts are my thoughts, *hozhoni, hozhoni*
The Earth, its speech is my speech, *hozhoni, hozhoni*
The sky, its life am I, *hozhoni, hozhoni*—
The mountains, its life am I—
The Sun, its life am I—
White corn, its life am I—
Yellow corn, its life am I—

The corn beetle, its life am I—
Hozhoni, hozhoni, hozhoni
Hozhoni, hozhoni, hozhoni
　　　Navaho chant

I am blind and do not see the things of this world; but when the light comes from above, it enlightens my heart and I can see, for the Eye of my heart sees everything; and through this vision I can help my people. The heart is a sanctuary at the center of which there is a little space, wherein the Great Spirit dwells, and this is the Eye. This is the Eye of the Great Spirit by which He sees all things, and through which we see Him. If the heart is not pure, the Great Spirit cannot be seen.
　　　Black Elk

. . . Then I sought solitude, and here I soon became very melancholy. I would sometimes fall to weeping, and feel unhappy without knowing why. Then for no reason, all would suddenly be changed, and I felt a great, inexplicable joy, a joy so powerful that I could not restrain it, but had to break into song, a mighty song, with only room for the one word: joy, joy! And I had to use the full strength of my voice. And then in the midst of such a fit of mysterious and overwhelming delight I became a shaman. I could see and hear in a totally different way. I had gained my *quameneq*, my enlightenment, the shaman-light of brain and body, and this in such a manner that it was not only I who could see through the darkness of life, but the same light also shone out from me, imperceptible to human beings, but visible to all the spirits of earth and sky and sea, and these now came to me and became my helping spirits.
　　　An Eskimo shaman

Remember, remember the sacredness of things
Running streams and dwellings
The young within the nest
A hearth for sacred fire
The holy flame of fire
　　　Pawnee song

Tree . . .
he watching you.
You look at tree,
he listen to you.
He got no finger,
he can't speak.
But that leaf . . .
he pumping, growing,
growing in the night.
While you sleeping
you dream something.
Tree and grass same thing.
They grow with your body,
with your feeling.

Aborigine song

Every part of this soil is sacred in the estimation of my people.
Every hillside, every valley, every plain and grove, has been
made holy by some sad or happy event in days long vanished.
Even the rocks, which seem to be voiceless and dead as they
swelter in the sun along the silent shore, thrill with memories of
stirring events connected with the lives of my people. And the
very dust upon which you now stand responds more lovingly to
their footsteps than to yours, because it is rich with the blood
of our ancestors and our bare feet are conscious of the sympa-
thetic touch.

Chief Seathl

You ask me to plow the ground. Shall I take a knife and tear
my mother's breast? Then when I die she will not take me to
her bosom to rest.

You ask me to dig for stone. Shall I dig under her skin for
bones? Then when I die I cannot enter her body to be born
again.

You ask me to cut grass and make hay and sell it, and be
rich like white men. But how dare I cut off my mother's hair?

Smohalla

O Great Spirit

Whose voice speaks in the winds,
and in the trees
whose breath gives life to all the world.
Listen to Your creature!
Hear me!
I am small and weak.
I need Your power.
I need Your wisdom.
Let me walk in beauty,
    and let my eyes be glad
    beholding the red and purple dawn.
Make my hands touch all things
You have made
with love,
and help my ears to hear Your voice
    in everything.
Make me wise
that I may understand
the sacred teachings
You have taught;
Help me learn the lessons hidden
    in every leaf and every stone.
    O Wakan-Tanka,
I need power
    not to be greater than my relations
    but to conquer the enemy in myself.
Make me ready to come to You always
    with a pure heart
    and with clear eyes,
So when the time comes for my life to fade away,
    as the sunset fades,
So may my spirit come to You
    with honor and without shame.
                From a traditional Native American prayer

Lady of all powers,
In whom light appears,
Radiant one
Beloved of Heaven and Earth,
Tiara-crowned
Priestess of the Highest God,
My Lady, you are the guardian
Of all greatness.
Your hand holds the seven powers:
You lift the powers of being,
You have hung them over your fingers,
You have gathered the many powers,
You have clasped them now
Like necklaces onto your breast.

What once was chanted of Nanna
Let it now be yours—
That you are as lofty as Heaven,
Let it be known!
That you devastate the rebellious,
Let it be known!
That you roared at the land,
Let it be known!
That you rain your blows on their heads,
Let it be known!
That you feast on corpses like a dog,
Let it be known!
That your glance is lifting toward them,
Let it be known!
That your glance is like striking lightning,
Let it be known!
That you are victorious,
Let it be known!
That this is not said of Nanna,
It is said of you—
This is your greatness.
You alone are the High One.

Enheduanna, from the Hymn to Inanna

The council of the animals met in the eternal darkness with hopes of finding a solution to the constant night—and to the difficulties of seeing the very ground on which they walked. Many tried to solve the problem. Rabbit dreamed up a plan—that didn't work. Fox devised another—that ended in failure. Eagle tried to find light—only to throw his wings up in discouragement. Woodpecker thought he could do better—only to find that the new world still remained in darkness.

After each had bragged in loud voices, and after each had failed, there was silence. Then from the darkness came a voice, a little voice that sounded very old. It was Spider Grandmother, suggesting that she might be able to remedy the problem. The others responded with laughter and challenging jeers. Surely this old grandmother could not do what Fox and Eagle could not do. But the wisdom of patience made her deaf to their answers. In hope of helping her people out of the blinding darkness, Spider Grandmother set off toward the East, set off toward the land of the Sun People.

The walk was long and arduous. Over vast dry deserts, over perilous mountain trails, across wide rivers and around wide lakes, Spider Grandmother continued to walk—the thread of her webbing spinning out behind her. In the darkness, she came upon a bed of soft wet clay and from it she fashioned a bowl. Once again, she began to walk, now carrying the new bowl in her hands. Many nights of darkness passed. Many days of darkness passed. And then a glow of orange appeared before her in the distance, telling her that she had reached the land of the Sun People.

Fatigued from the long walk, she rested, not far from the blazing fire that wondrously lit the night—hoping that she would not be noticed. As the evening went by, closer and closer she drew to the great fire that lit the land of the Sun People. And then, so quickly that no one saw, she pinched off a small piece of the bright orange flame, popped it into her bowl, and walked quietly away.

Following the strand of web that she had spun behind her, Spider Grandmother began the long walk home. She carried the bowl with great care, so that the piece of fire would not fall out. But much to her surprise, the fire grew brighter and larger as she walked, until its brightness and its heat became so unbearably intense that she flung the blazing fireball into the air. Tiny and old as she was, she flung the fire so high up into the heavens that it stayed there and became the sun. So it was that Spider Grandmother brought light for her people, ending the darkness that had been in the New World.

Yet even at the moment that she tossed the sun into the sky, Spider Grandmother thought to keep a small piece. This she placed in the bowl and brought back to her people, giving them this second gift of fire for the cooking of the food, for the baking of the clay and for the light of the evening campfire. It is no wonder that when people, even today, sit about the council fire, they tell these and other wondrous stories of the ancient Spider Grandmother.

Native American myth

TRUTH

Osa-Otura says, What is truth?

I say, What is truth?

Orunmila says: Truth is the Lord of heaven guiding the earth.

Osa-Otura says, What is truth?

I say, What is truth?

Orunmila says: Truth is the unseen One guiding the earth, the wisdom Olodumare is using—great wisdom, many wisdoms.

Osa-Otura says, What is truth?

I say, What is truth?

Orunmila says: Truth is the character of Olodumare. Truth is the word that cannot fall. Ifa is truth. Truth is the word that cannot spoil. Mighty power, surpassing all. Everlasting blessing.

This was divined for the earth. They said the people in the world should be truthful. . . .

Ifa song: Speak the truth, tell the facts. Speak the truth, tell the facts. Those who speak the truth are those whom the deity will help.

From the African Ifa Oracle

Grandfather,
Look at our brokenness.
We know that in all creation
Only the human family
Has strayed from the Sacred Way.
We know that we are the ones
Who are divided
And we are the ones
Who must come back together
To walk in the Sacred Way.
Grandfather,
Sacred One,
Teach us love, compassion, and honor
That we may heal the earth
And heal each other.
    Ojibway prayer

THE TRUE PEACE

The first peace, which is the most important, is that which
comes within the souls of men when they realize their relationship, their oneness, with the universe and all its powers, and
when they realize that at the center of the universe dwells
Wakan-Tanka, and that this center is really everywhere, it is
within each of us. This is the real peace, and the others are but
reflections of this. The second peace is that which is made between two individuals, and the third is that which is made
between two nations. But above all you should understand
that there can never be peace between nations until there
is first known that true peace, which, as I have often said,
is within the souls of men.
    Black Elk

Power is not manifested in the human being. True power is in
the Creator. If we continue to ignore the message by which we
exist and we continue to destroy the source of our lives, then
our children will suffer. . . . I must warn you that the Creator
made us all equal with one another. And not only human beings, but all life is equal. The equality of our life is what you
must understand and the principles by which you must con-

tinue on behalf of the future of this world. Economics and technology may assist you, but they will also destroy you if you do not use the principles of equality. Profit and loss will mean nothing to your future generations. . . .

I do not see a delegation for the four-footed. I see no seat for the eagles. We forget and we consider ourselves superior, but we are after all a mere part of the Creation. And we must continue to understand where we are. And we stand between the mountain and the ant, somewhere and there only, as part and parcel of the Creation. It is our responsibility, since we have been given the minds to take care of these things. The elements and the animals, and the birds, they live in a state of grace. They are absolute, they can do no wrong. It is only we, the two-leggeds, that can do this. And when we do this to our brothers, to our own brothers, then we do the worst in the eyes of the Creator.

> *Oren Lyons, from an address given to the United Nations (1977)*

Dark young pine, at the center of the earth originating,
I have made your sacrifice.
Whiteshell, turquoise, abalone beautiful,
Jet beautiful, fool's gold beautiful, blue pollen beautiful,
Reed pollen, pollen beautiful, your sacrifice I have made.
This day your child I have become, I say.

Watch over me.
Hold your hand before me in protection.
Stand guard for me, speak in defense of me.
As I speak for you, speak for me.
  May it be beautiful before me.
  May it be beautiful behind me.
  May it be beautiful below me.
  May it be beautiful above me,
  May it be beautiful all around me.

I am restored in beauty.
I am restored in beauty.
I am restored in beauty.
I am restored in beauty.

> *Traditional Navaho prayer*

ふ

Taoism
The Way of the Tao

Of all the world's great mystical systems, it is Taoism—the earliest knowledge tradition of China—that has preserved most subtly and comprehensively that original sense of unity with Being that we find in the "voices of the first world." According to tradition, Taoism originated with a man called Lao Tzu, sometimes translated as "Old Boy" or "Old Child," who is said to have been born in the sixth century B.C. and to have written his classic, *Tao Te Ching*, "The Way and Its Power," in three days in late old age before riding off into the mountains of Tibet.

The concept around which all of Taoist mystical philosophy revolves is the infinitely mysterious one of the Tao. The Tao is at once the "Way of Final Reality," the transcendent womb out of which all things are born, by which they are sustained, and into which they die; the "Way of the Universe," the rhythm, creative force, and subtle dance of nature and the ordering principle behind all life; and the "Way of Authentic Human Life," of that living in tune with the mystery that is balanced, peaceful, reverent, joyful, and simple in all its claims, needs, and habits.

Taoists honor balance above all and the masculine yang energy, but they are aware that it is through what the *Tao Te Ching* calls the valley spirit—the spirit of the sacred feminine, the Mother, the yin energy—that the deepest realization is attained. No other mystical tradition has celebrated the humbling, nourishing, unitive powers of the sacred feminine so adamantly:

Know the male, keep the female;
Be humble toward the world.
Be humble toward the world,
And eternal power never leaves.

From this feminine "humility toward the world" springs, the Taoists tell us, a magical spontaneity they name *tzu jan,* the wholly natural joy of the free being who has learned how to rest in the fecund silence of the Tao and who is forever free of the need to accumulate possessions or power of any kind. At home in the dark as well as the light, earth as well as heaven, yin as well as yang, death as well as life, the Taoist adept at one with the Tao learns to be at peace in the universe and to act in life with the calm, freedom, abandon, and radical egalitarian simplicity and tolerance of the Tao itself, knowing in Chuang Tzu's words "that the ten thousand things belong to one storehouse and life and death share the same body." Any action undertaken from this position of mysterious freedom and balance will naturally radiate mystic power, because it will be filled with the power of the Tao itself and in harmony with it.

This vision in its sanity, lack of pretension, depth, humanity, and wise, demanding humility offers, I have found, a marvelous touchstone by which to inwardly test both the truths and the imbalances of the later mystical traditions.

Multiply the efforts of the ordinary person a hundredfold, and you can actually master this Tao. Even if you are ignorant you will become enlightened, even if you are weak you will become strong—no one who has done this has ever failed to reach the realm of profound attainment of self-realization.
  Liu I Ming

Master Tung-kuo asked Chuang Tzu, "This thing called the Way—where does it exist?"

Chuang Tzu said, "There's no place it doesn't exist."

"Come," said Master Tung-kuo, "you must be more specific!"

"It is in the ant."

"As low a thing as that?"

"It is in the panic grass."

"But that's lower still!"

"It is in the tiles and shards."

"How can it be so low?"

"It is in the piss and dung."
  Chuang Tzu

1. A Way Can Be a Guide

A way can be a guide, but not a fixed path;
names can be given, but not permanent labels.
Nonbeing is called the beginning of heaven and earth;
being is called the mother of all things.
Always passionless, thereby observe the subtle;
ever intent, thereby observe the apparent.
These two come from the same source but differ in name;
both are considered mysteries.
The mystery of mysteries
is the gateway of marvels.

4. The Way Is Unimpeded Harmony

The Way is unimpeded harmony;
its potential may never be fully exploited.
It is as deep as the source of all things:
it blunts the edges,
resolves the complications,
harmonizes the light,
assimilates to the world.
Profoundly still, it seems to be there:
I don't know whose child it is,
before the creation of images.

6. The Valley Spirit

The valley spirit not dying
is called the mysterious female.
The opening of the mysterious female
is called the root of heaven and earth.
Continuous, on the brink of existence,
to put it into practice, don't try to force it.

10. Carrying Vitality and Consciousness

Carrying vitality and consciousness,
embracing them as one,

can you keep them from parting?
Concentrating energy,
making it supple,
can you be like an infant?
Purifying hidden perception,
can you make it flawless?
Loving the people, governing the nation,
can you be uncontrived?
As the gate of heaven opens and closes,
can you be impassive?
As understanding reaches everywhere,
can you be innocent?
Producing and developing,
producing without possessing,
doing without presuming,
growing without domineering:
this is called mysterious power.

16. Attain the Climax of Emptiness

Attain the climax of emptiness,
preserve the utmost quiet:
as myriad things act in concert,
I thereby observe the return.
Things flourish,
then each returns to its root.
Returning to the root is called stillness:
stillness is called return to Life,
return to Life is called the constant;
knowing the constant is called enlightenment.
Acts at random, in ignorance of the constant, bode ill.
Knowing the constant gives perspective;
this perspective is impartial.
Impartiality is the highest nobility;
the highest nobility is divine,
and the divine is the Way.
This Way is everlasting,
not endangered by physical death.

19. Eliminate Sagacity, Abandon Knowledge

Eliminate sagacity, abandon knowledge,
and the people benefit a hundredfold.
Eliminate humanitarianism, abandon duty,
and the people return to familial love.
Eliminate craft, abandon profit,
and theft will no longer exist.
These three become insufficient
when used for embellishment
causing there to be attachments.
See the basic,
embrace the unspoiled,
lessen selfishness,
diminish desire.

20. Detach from Learning and You Have No Worries

Detach from learning and you have no worries.
How far apart are yes and yeah?
How far apart are good and bad?
The things people fear cannot but be feared.
Wild indeed the uncentered!
Most people celebrate
as if they were barbecuing a slaughtered cow,
or taking in the springtime vistas;
I alone am aloof,
showing no sign,
like an infant that doesn't yet smile,
riding buoyantly
as if with nowhere to go.
Most people have too much;
I alone seem to be missing something.
Mine is indeed the mind of an ignoramus
in its unadulterated simplicity.
Ordinary people try to shine;
I alone seem to be dark.
Ordinary people try to be on the alert;
I alone am unobtrusive,

calm as the ocean depths,
buoyant as if anchored nowhere.
Most people have ways and means;
I alone am unsophisticated and simple.
I alone am different from people
in that I value seeking food from the mother.

25. Something Undifferentiated

Something undifferentiated was born before heaven and
earth;
still and silent, standing alone and unchanging,
going through cycles unending,
able to be mother to the world.
I do not know its name;
I label it the Way.
Imposing on it a name,
I call it Great.
Greatness means it goes;
going means reaching afar;
reaching afar means return.
Therefore the Way is great,
heaven is great,
earth is great,
and kingship is also great.
Among domains are four greats,
of which kingship is one.
Humanity emulates earth,
earth emulates heaven,
heaven emulates the Way,
the Way emulates Nature.

28. Know the Male

Know the male, keep the female;
be humble toward the world.
Be humble toward the world,
and eternal power never leaves,
returning again to innocence.

Knowing the white, keep the black;
be an exemplar for the world.
Be an exemplar for the world,
and eternal power never goes awry,
returning again to infinity.
Knowing the glorious, keep the ignominious;
be open to the world.
Be open to the world,
and eternal power suffices,
returning again to simplicity.
Simplicity is lost to make instruments,
which sages employ as functionaries.
Therefore the great fashioner does no splitting.

39. Ancient Attainment of Unity

When unity was attained of old,
heaven became clear by attaining unity,
earth became steady by attaining unity,
spirit was quickened by attaining unity,
valley streams were filled by attaining unity,
all beings were born by attaining unity;
and by attaining unity lords acted rightly
for the sake of the world.
What brought this about was unity:
without means of clarity, heaven may burst;
without means of steadiness, earth may erupt;
without means of quickening, spirit may be exhausted;
without means of filling, valley streams may dry up;
without means of birth, all beings may perish;
without means of acting rightly, lords may stumble.
Therefore nobility is rooted in humility,
loftiness is based on lowliness.
This is why noble people refer to themselves
as alone, lacking, and unworthy.
Is this not being rooted in humility?
So there is no praise in repeated praise;
they don't want to be like jewels or like stones.

41. *When Superior People Hear of the Way*

When superior people hear of the Way,
they carry it out with diligence.
When middling people hear of the Way,
it sometimes seems to be there, sometimes not.
When lesser people hear of the Way,
they ridicule it greatly.
If they didn't laugh at it,
it wouldn't be the Way.
So there are constructive sayings on this:
The Way of illumination seems dark,
the Way of advancement seems retiring,
the Way of equality seems to categorize;
higher virtue seems empty,
great purity seems ignominious,
broad virtue seems insufficient,
constructive virtue seems careless.
Simple honesty seems changeable,
great range has no boundaries,
great vessels are finished late;
the great sound has a rarefied tone,
the great image has no form,
the Way hides in namelessness.
Only the Way can enhance and perfect.

52. *The World Has a Beginning*

The world has a beginning
that is the mother of the world.
Once you've found the mother,
thereby you know the child.
Once you know the child,
you return to keep the mother,
not perishing though the body die.
Close your eyes, shut your doors,
and you do not toil all your life.
Open your eyes, carry out your affairs,
and you are not saved all your life.

Seeing the small is called clarity;
keeping flexible is called strength.
Using the shining radiance,
you return again to the light,
not leaving anything to harm yourself.
This is called entering the eternal.

67. *Everyone Says*

Everyone in the world
says my Way is great,
but it seems incomparable.
It is just because it is great
that it seems incomparable:
when comparisons are long established
it becomes trivialized.

I have three treasures
that I keep and hold:
one is mercy,
the second is frugality,
the third is not presuming
to be at the head of the world.
By reason of mercy,
one can be brave.
By reason of frugality,
one can be broad.
By not presuming
to be at the head of the world,
one can make your potential last.

Now if one were bold
but had no mercy,
if one were broad
but were not frugal,
if one went ahead
without deference,
one would die.

Use mercy in war,
and you win;
use it for defense,
and you're secure.
Those whom heaven is going to save
are those it guards with mercy.

78. *The Most Flexible Thing in the World*

Nothing in the world is more flexible
and yielding than water.
Yet when it attacks the firm and the strong,
none can withstand it,
because they have no way to change it.
So the flexible overcome the adamant,
the yielding overcome the forceful.
Everyone knows this,
but no one can do it.
This is why sages say
those who can take on the disgrace of nations
are leaders of lands;
those who can take on the misfortune of nations
are rulers of the world.
True sayings seem paradoxical.

79. *Harmonize Bitter Enemies*

When you harmonize bitter enemies,
yet resentment is sure to linger,
how can this be called good?
Therefore sages keep their faith
and do not pressure others.
So the virtuous see to their promises,
while the virtueless look after precedents.
The Way of heaven is impersonal;
it is always with good people.
> *Lao Tzu, from the* Tao Te Ching

I'm going to try speaking some reckless words and I want you to listen to them recklessly. . . .

"How do I know that loving life is not a delusion? How do I know that in hating death I am not like a man who, having left home in his youth, has forgotten the way back?

"Lady Li was the daughter of the border guard of Ai. When she was first taken captive and brought to the state of Chin, she wept until her tears drenched the collar of her robe. But later, when she went to live in the palace of the ruler, shared his couch with him, and ate the delicious meats of his table, she wondered why she had ever wept. How do I know that the dead do not wonder why they ever longed for life?

"He who dreams of drinking wine may weep when morning comes; he who dreams of weeping may in the morning go off to hunt. While he is dreaming he does not know it is a dream, and in his dream he may even try to interpret a dream. Only after he wakes does he know it was a dream. And someday there will be a great awakening when we know that this is all a great dream. Yet the stupid believe they are awake, busily and brightly assuming they understand things, calling this man ruler, that one herdsman—how dense! Confucius and you are both dreaming! And when I say you are dreaming, I am dreaming, too. Words like these will be labeled the Supreme Swindle. Yet, after ten thousand generations, a great sage may appear who will know their meaning, and it will still be as though he appeared with astonishing speed."

Chuang Tzu

THE SECRET OF CARING FOR LIFE

Cook Ting was cutting up an ox for Lord Wen-hui. At every touch of his hand, every heave of his shoulder, every move of his feet, every thrust of his knee—zip! zoop! He slithered the knife along with a zing, and all was in perfect rhythm, as though he were performing the dance of the Mulberry Grove or keeping time to the Ching-shou music.

"Ah, this is marvelous!" said Lord Wen-hui. "Imagine skill reaching such heights!"

Cook Ting laid down his knife and replied, "What I care about is the Way, which goes beyond skill. When I first began cutting up oxen, all I could see was the ox itself. After three years I no longer saw the whole ox. And now—now I go at it by spirit and don't look with my eyes. Perception and understanding have come to a stop and spirit moves where it wants. I go along with the natural makeup, strike in the big hollows, guide the knife through the big openings, and follow things as they are. So I never touch the smallest ligament or tendon, much less a main joint.

"A good cook changes his knife once a year—because he cuts. A mediocre cook changes his knife once a month—because he hacks. I've had this knife of mine for nineteen years and I've cut up thousands of oxen with it, and yet the blade is as good as though it had just come from the grindstone. There are spaces between the joints, and the blade of the knife has really no thickness. If you insert what has no thickness into such spaces, then there's plenty of room—more than enough for the blade to play about in. That's why after nineteen years the blade of my knife is still as good as when it first came from the grindstone.

"However, whenever I come to a complicated place, I size up the difficulties, tell myself to watch out and be careful, keep my eyes on what I'm doing, work very slowly, and move the knife with the greatest subtlety, until—flop! the whole thing comes apart like a clod of earth crumbling to the ground. I stand there holding the knife and look all around me, completely satisfied and reluctant to move on, and then I wipe off the knife and put it away."

"Excellent!" said Lord Wen-hui. "I have heard the words of Cook Ting and learned how to care for life!"

Chuang Tzu

THE TRUE MAN

What do I mean by a True Man? The True Man of ancient times did not rebel against want, did not grow proud in plenty, and did not plan his affairs. Being like this, he could commit an error and not regret it, could meet with success and not make a show. Being like this, he could climb the high places and not be frightened, could enter the water and not get wet, could enter the fire and not get burned. His knowledge was able to climb all the way up to the Way like this.

The True Man of ancient times slept without dreaming and woke without care; he ate without savoring and his breath came from deep inside. The True Man breathes with his heels; the mass of men breathe with their throats. Crushed and bound down, they gasp out their words as though they were retching. Deep in their passions and desires, they are shallow in the workings of Heaven.

The True Man of ancient times knew nothing of loving life, knew nothing of hating death. He emerged without delight; he went back in without a fuss. He came briskly, he went briskly, and that was all. He didn't forget where he began; he didn't try to find out where he would end. He received something and took pleasure in it; he forgot about it and handed it back again. This is what I call not using the mind to repel the Way, not using man to help out Heaven. This is what I call the True Man.

Chuang Tzu

Master Lieh Tzu said to the Barrier Keeper Yin, "The Perfect Man can walk under water without choking, can tread on fire without being burned, and can travel above the ten thousand things without being frightened. May I ask how he manages this?"

The Barrier Keeper Yin replied, "This is because he guards the pure breath—it has nothing to do with wisdom, skill, determination, or courage. Sit down and I will tell you about it. All that have faces, forms, voices, colors—these are all mere things. How could one thing and another thing be far removed from each other? And how could any of them be capable of leading you to what preceded them? They are forms, colors—nothing more. But that which creates things has no form, and it rests where there is no change. If a man can get hold of this and exhaust it fully, then how can things stand in his way? He may rest within the bounds that know no excess, hide within the borders that know no source, wander where the ten thousand things have their end and beginning, unify his nature, nourish his breath, unite his virtue, and thereby communicate with that which creates all things. A man like this guards what belongs to Heaven and keeps it whole. His spirit has no flaw, so how can things enter in and get at him?

"When a drunken man falls from a carriage, though the carriage may be going very fast, he won't be killed. He has bones and joints the same as other men, and yet he is not injured as they would be, because his spirit is whole. He didn't know he was riding, and he doesn't know he has fallen out. Life and death, alarm and terror do not enter his breast, and so he can bang against things without fear of injury. If he can keep himself whole like this by means of wine, how much more can he keep himself whole by means of Heaven! The sage hides himself in Heaven—hence there is nothing that can do him harm.

Chuang Tzu

Chi Hsing-tzu was training gamecocks for the king. After ten days the king asked if they were ready.

"Not yet. They're too taught to rely on their nerve."

Another ten days and the king asked again.

"Not yet. They still respond to noises and movements."

Another ten days and the king asked again.

"Not yet. They still look around fiercely and are full of spirit."

Another ten days and the king asked again.

"They're close enough. Another cock can crow and they show no sign of change. Look at them from a distance and you'd think they were made of wood. Their virtue is complete. Other cocks won't dare face up to them, but will turn and run."

Chuang Tzu

MYSTIC ADVICE

Man has received from heaven a nature innately good, to guide him in all his movements. By devotion to this divine spirit within himself, he attains an unsullied innocence that leads him to do right with instinctive sureness and without any ulterior thought of reward and personal advantage. This instinctive certainty brings about supreme success and "furthers through perseverance." However, not everything instinctive is nature in this higher sense of the word, but only that which is right and in accord with the will of heaven. Without this quality of rightness, an unreflecting, instinctive way of acting brings only misfortune. Confucius says about this: "He who departs from innocence, what does he come to? Heaven's will and blessing do not go with his deeds."

In a resolute struggle of the good against evil, there are, however, definite rules that must not be disregarded, if it is to succeed. First, resolution must be based on a union of strength and friendliness. Second, a compromise with evil is not possible; evil must under all circumstances be openly discredited. Nor must our own passions and shortcomings be glossed over. Third, the struggle must not be carried on directly by force. If evil is branded, it thinks of weapons, and if we do it the favor of fighting against it blow for blow, we lose in the end because thus we ourselves get entangled in hatred and passion. Therefore it is important to begin at home, to be on guard in our own persons against the faults we have branded. In this way, finding no opponent, the sharp edges of the weapons of evil become dulled. For the same reasons we should not combat our own faults directly. As long as we wrestle with them, they continue victorious. Finally, the best way to fight evil is to make energetic progress in the good.

Hexagrams 25, 43, from the I Ching

THE HEIGHT OF HEAVEN, THE THICKNESS OF EARTH

The body of heaven is extremely high. Open, round, immeasurable, it is boundlessly vast. Covering everything, containing everything, it produces myriad beings without presuming on its virtue, it bestows blessings on myriad beings without expectation of reward. Whether people are respectful or insincere, supportive or antagonistic is left up to them. Whether people are good or bad, attractive or repulsive, and whether creatures are violent and stubborn or docile and obedient, they are allowed to be so of themselves, without any contrivance.

The earth is very thick. Lowly, below all else, it bears everything and nurtures all beings. It can bear even the weight of the great mountains, and it can endure even the erosive force of great waters. It tolerates being pierced by plants and trees, and it submits to the tread of birds and beasts.

What I realize as I observe this is the Tao of emulating heaven and earth. If people can be open-minded and magnanimous, be receptive to all, take pity on the old and the poor, assist those in peril and rescue those in trouble, give of themselves without seeking reward, never bear grudges, look upon others and self impartially, and realize all as one, then people can be companions of heaven.

If people can be flexible and yielding, humble, with self-control, entirely free of agitation, cleared of all volatility, not angered by criticism, ignoring insult, docilely accepting all hardships, illnesses, and natural disasters, utterly without anxiety or resentment when faced with danger or adversity, then people can be companions of the earth.

With the nobility of heaven and the humility of earth, one joins in with the attributes of heaven and earth and extends to eternity with them.

Liu I Ming

To know Tao
meditate
and still the mind.
Knowledge comes with perseverance.

The Way is neither full nor empty;
a modest and quiet nature understands this.
The empty vessel, the uncarved block;
nothing is more mysterious.

When enlightenment arrives
don't talk too much about it;
just live it in your own way.
With humility and depth, rewards come naturally.

The fragrance of blossoms soon passes;
the ripeness of fruit is gone in a twinkling.
Our time in this world is so short,
better to avoid regret:
Miss no opportunity to savor the ineffable.

Like a golden beacon signaling on a moonless night,
Tao guides our passage through this transitory realm.
In moments of darkness and pain
remember all is cyclical.
Sit quietly behind your wooden door:
Spring will come again.
      Loy Ching Yuen

3

Hinduism
The Way of Presence

The name Hindus give to that ultimate reality that is forever nameless and formless and beyond definition is "Brahman." The Sanskrit word has a dual etymology, deriving at once from *br*, "to breathe," and *brih*, "to be great." The chief attributes of Brahman are *Sat*, *Chit*, and *Ananda*, roughly translated as Being, Awareness, and Bliss. Absolute reality is conceived by the Hindu mind as being a Presence of Pure Being, Pure Consciousness, and Pure Bliss. All the different "gods" represent "modes" of this one reality's working; behind all multiplicity in Hinduism, however fantastic and baroque, there is always the underlying indivisible and eternal unity of all things.

For the Hindu mystic, every human being is one with Brahman in his or her Atman—his or her divine self or soul. The aim of human life is to know the Atman consciously and to live the calm, fearless, and selflessly loving life that arises from this knowledge.

Hinduism acknowledges the differences in people's personalities and religious temperaments and takes a marvelously and ripely practical attitude to attaining union with the Atman-Brahman. Four main paths of *yoga* ("union with God") were gradually developed to suit different ways of imagining, approaching, and enacting the divine: *jnana yoga,* the path to the transcendent through knowledge; *bhakti yoga*, the path of devotion, usually to a "personal" god; *raja yoga*, the path of royal (*raj*) reintegration through psychophysical exercises; and *karma yoga*, the path of works and action dedicated selflessly to the Supreme.

Along with its faith in the grandeur of the divine self and its tolerance, Hinduism's chief attraction to us now is that it has kept alive a very full at once majestic and tender vision of God the Mother, of God as divine Mother. The Hindu vision of the Mother (known in many different aspects and names) has nothing whatever to do with the largely passive version of her we meet, for example, in traditional Catholicism. The Hindus know the Mother in her full power and glory, as Destroyer as well as Preserver, as "terrible" as well as "tender," as nothing less than the active side of Brahman itself, the force, or Shakti, of Brahman, that is, the force that creates, sustains, destroys, and remakes all things. The beauty of this immense cosmic vision of the Mother is that it is also one of complete intimacy; the Mother is known as all-loving as well as all-powerful, totally attentive to every thing and being in creation, and contactable anywhere and at any time by her children.

It is this vision of the Mother that her greatest modern "children" Ramakrishna and Aurobindo have elaborated to enlarge and correct some of the world- and body-denying tendencies that developed within traditional Hinduism. Ramakrishna took Hindu tolerance to the extreme of a love embracing all paths, religions, and beings; Aurobindo "discovered" the Mother as that force that wills a new transformed humanity on earth and can, with our cooperation, create it.

> Lead me from the unreal to the real.
> Lead me from darkness to light.
> Lead me from death to immortality.
>   *Upanishad invocation*

Once Bhrigu Varuni went to his father, Varuna, and said: "Father, explain to me the mystery of Brahman."

Then his father spoke to him of the food of the earth, of the breath of life, of the one who sees, of the one who hears, of the mind that knows, and of the one who speaks. And he further said to him: "Seek to know him from whom all beings have come, by whom they all live, and unto whom they all return. He is Brahman."

So Bhrigu went and practiced *tapas*, spiritual prayer. Then he thought that Brahman was the food of the earth: for from the earth all beings have come, by food of the earth they all live, and unto the earth they all return.

After this he went again to his father, Varuna, and said: "Father, explain further to me the mystery of Brahman." To him his father answered: "Seek to know Brahman by *tapas*, by prayer, because Brahman is prayer."

So Bhrigu went and practiced *tapas*, spiritual prayer. Then he thought that Brahman was life: for from life all beings have come, by life they all live, and unto life they all return.

After this he went again to his father, Varuna, and said: "Father, explain further to me the mystery of Brahman." To him his father answered: "Seek to know Brahman by *tapas*, by prayer, because Brahman is prayer."

So Bhrigu went and practiced *tapas*, spiritual prayer. Then he thought that Brahman was mind: for from mind all beings have come, by mind they all live, and unto mind they all return.

After this he went again to his father, Varuna, and said: "Father, explain further to me the mystery of Brahman." To him his father answered: "Seek to know Brahman by *tapas,* by prayer, because Brahman is prayer."

So Bhrigu went and practiced *tapas*, spiritual prayer. Then he thought that Brahman was reason: for from reason all beings have come, by reason they all live, and unto reason they all return.

He went again to his father, asked the same question, and received the same answer.

So Bhrigu went and practiced *tapas,* spiritual prayer. And then he saw that Brahman is joy: for *from joy all beings have come, by joy they all live, and unto joy they all return.*

This was the vision of Bhrigu Varuni which came from the Highest; and he who sees this vision lives in the Highest.

From the Taittiriya Upanishad

THE CITY OF BRAHMAN \

In the city of Brahman is a secret dwelling,
the lotus of the heart. Within this dwelling
is a space, and within that space is the
fulfillment of our desires. What is within
that space should be longed for and realized.

As great as the infinite space beyond is the
space within the lotus of the heart. Both
heaven and earth are contained in that inner
space, both fire and air, sun and moon,
lightning and stars. Whether we know it
in this world or know it not, everything is
contained in that inner space.

Never fear that old age will invade that
city; never fear that this inner treasure of all
reality will wither and decay. This knows
no age when the body ages; this knows no
dying when the body dies. This is the real
city of Brahman; this is the Self, free from
old age, from death and grief, hunger and
thirst. In the Self all desires are fulfilled.

> *From the* Chandogya Upanishad

YOU ARE THAT

This is the teaching of Uddalaka to Shvetaketu, his son:

As by knowing one lump of clay, dear one,
We come to know all things made out of clay—
That they differ only in name and form,
While the stuff of which all are made is clay;

As by knowing one gold nugget, dear one,
We come to know all things made out of gold—
That they differ only in name and form,
While the stuff of which all are made is gold;

As by knowing one tool of iron, dear one,
We come to know all things made out of iron—
That they differ only in name and form,
While the stuff of which all are made is iron—

So through spiritual wisdom, dear one,
We come to know that all of life is one.

In the beginning was only Being,
One without a second.

Out of himself he brought forth the cosmos)
And entered into everything in it.)
There is nothing that does not come from him.
Of everything he is the inmost Self.
He is the truth; he is the Self supreme.
You are that, Shvetaketu; you are that.

From the Chandogya Upanishad

The Spirit, without moving, is swifter than the mind; the senses cannot reach him: He is ever beyond them. Standing still, he overtakes those who run. To the ocean of his being, the spirit of life leads the streams of action.

He moves, and he moves not. He is far, and he is near. He is within all, and he is outside all.

Who sees all beings in his own Self, and his own Self in all beings, loses all fear.

When a sage sees this great Unity and his Self has become all beings, what delusion and what sorrow can ever be near him?

The Spirit filled all with his radiance. He is incorporeal and invulnerable, pure and untouched by evil. He is the supreme seer and thinker, immanent and transcendent. He placed all things in the path of Eternity.

Into deep darkness fall those who follow action. Into deeper darkness fall those who follow knowledge.

One is the outcome of knowledge, and another is the outcome of action. Thus have we heard from the ancient sages who explained this truth to us.

He who knows both knowledge and action, with action overcomes death and with knowledge reaches immortality.

Into deep darkness fall those who follow the immanent. Into deeper darkness fall those who follow the transcendent.

One is the outcome of the transcendent, and another is the outcome of the immanent. Thus have we heard from the ancient sages who explained this truth to us.

He who knows both the transcendent and the immanent, with the immanent overcomes death and with the transcendent reaches immortality.

From the Isa Upanishad

All is change in the world of the senses,
But changeless is the supreme Lord of Love.
Meditate on him, be absorbed in him,
Wake up from this dream of separateness.

Know God and all fetters will fall away.
No longer identifying yourself
With the body, go beyond birth and death.
All your desires will be fulfilled in him
Who is One without a second.

Know him to be enshrined within your heart
Always. Truly there is nothing more
To know in life. Meditate and realize
The world is filled with the presence of God.

Fire is not seen until one firestick rubs
Against another, though the fire remains
Hidden in the firestick. So does the Lord
Remain hidden in the body until
He is revealed through the mystic mantram.

Let your body be the lower firestick;
Let the mantram be the upper. Rub them
Against each other in meditation
And realize the Lord.

Like oil in sesame seeds, like butter
In cream, like water in springs, like fire
In a firestick, so dwells the Lord of Love,
The Self, in the very depths of consciousness.
Realize him through truth and meditation.

The Self is hidden in the hearts of all,
As butter lies hidden in cream. Realize
The Self in the depths of meditation,
The Lord of Love, supreme reality,
Who is the goal of all knowledge.

This is the highest mystical teaching;
This is the highest mystical teaching.

From the Shveteshvatara Upanishad

There are two birds, two sweet friends, who dwell on the self-same tree. The one eats the fruits hereof, and the other looks on in silence.

The first is the human soul who, resting on that tree, though active, feels sad in his unwisdom. But on beholding the power and glory of the higher Spirit, he becomes free from sorrow.

When the wise seer beholds in golden glory the Lord, the Spirit, the Creator of the god of creation, then he leaves good and evil behind and in purity he goes to the unity supreme.

In silent wonder the wise see him as the life flaming in all creation. This is the greatest seer of Brahman, who, doing all his work as holy work, in God, in Atman, in the Self, finds all his peace and joy. . . .

Not through much learning is the Atman reached, not through the intellect or sacred teaching. He is reached by the chosen of him. To his chosen the Atman reveals his glory.

The Atman is not reached by the weak, or the careless, or those who practice wrong austerity; but the wise who strive in the right way lead their soul into the dwelling of Brahman.

Having reached that place supreme, the seers find joy in wisdom, their souls have fulfillment, their passions have gone, they have peace. Filled with devotion, they have found the Spirit in all and go into the All.

From the Mundaka Upanishad

"Maitreyi," said one day Yajnavalkya to his wife, "I am going to leave this present life, and retire to a life of meditation. Let me settle my possessions upon you and Katyayani."

"If all the earth filled with riches belonged to me, O my Lord," said Maitreyi, "should I thereby attain life eternal?"

"Certainly not," said Yajnavalkya, "your life would only be as is the life of wealthy people. In wealth there is no hope of life eternal."

Maitreyi said: "What should I then do with possessions that cannot give me life eternal? Give me instead your knowledge, O my Lord."

On hearing this Yajnavalkya exclaimed: "Dear you are to me, beloved, and dear are the words you say. Come, sit down and I will teach; but hear my words with deep attention."

Then spoke Yajnavalkya:

"In truth, it is not for the love of a husband that a husband is dear; but for the love of the Soul in the husband that a husband is dear.

"It is not for the love of a wife that a wife is dear; but for the love of the Soul in the wife that a wife is dear.

"It is not for the love of children that children are dear; but for the love of the Soul in children that children are dear.

"It is not for the love of riches that riches are dear; but for the love of the Soul in riches that riches are dear.

"It is not for the love of religion that religion is dear; but for the love of the Soul in religion that religion is dear.

"It is not for the love of power that power is dear; but for the love of the Soul in power that power is dear.

"It is not for the love of the heavens that the heavens are dear; but for the love of the Soul in the heavens that the heavens are dear.

"It is not for the love of the gods that the gods are dear; but for the love of the Soul in the gods that the gods are dear.

"It is not for the love of creatures that creatures are dear; but for the love of the Soul in creatures that creatures are dear.

"It is not for the love of the all that the all is dear; but for the love of the Soul in the all that the all is dear.

"It is the Soul, the Spirit, the Self, that must be seen and be heard and have our thoughts and meditation, O Maitreyi. When the Soul is seen and heard, is thought upon and is known, then all that is becomes known.

"Religion will abandon the man who thinks that religion is apart from the Soul.

"Power will abandon the man who thinks that power is apart from the Soul.

"The gods will abandon the man who thinks that the gods are apart from the Soul.

"Creatures will abandon the man who thinks that creatures are apart from the Soul.

"And all will abandon the man who thinks that the all is apart from the Soul. Because religion, power, heavens, beings, gods and all rest on the Soul."

From the Brihad-Aranyaka Upanishad

Sri Krishna:
Those who are free from selfish attachments,
Who have mastered the senses and passions,
Act not, but are acted through by the Lord.
Listen to me now, O son of Kunti,
How one who has become an instrument
In the hands of the Lord attains Brahman,
The supreme consummation of wisdom.

Unerring in discrimination,
Sovereign of the senses and passions,
Free from the clamor of likes and dislikes,
They lead a simple, self-reliant life
Based on meditation, using speech,
Body, and mind to serve the Lord of Love.

Free from self-will, aggressiveness, arrogance,
From the lust to possess people or things,
They are at peace with themselves and others
And enter into the unitive state.

United with the Lord, ever joyful,
Beyond the reach of self-will and sorrow,
They serve me in every living creature
And attain supreme devotion to me.
By loving me they share in my glory
And enter into my boundless being.

All their acts are performed in my service,
And through my grace they win eternal life.

Make every act an offering to me;
Regard me as your only protector.
Make every thought an offering to me;
Meditate on me always.

Drawing upon your deepest resources,
You shall overcome all difficulties
Through my grace. But if you will not heed me
In your self-will, nothing will avail you.

If you say, "I will not fight this battle,"
Your own nature will drive you into it.
If you will not fight the battle of life,
Your own karma will drive you into it.

The Lord dwells in the hearts of all creatures,
And he whirls them round on the wheel of time.
Run to him for refuge with all your strength
And peace profound will be yours through his grace.

I give you these precious words of wisdom;
Reflect on them and then choose what is best. . . .

Be aware of me always, adore me,
Make every act an offering to me,
And you shall come to me;
This I promise, for you are dear to me.
Leave all other support, and look to me
For protection. I shall purify you
From the sins of the past. Do not grieve.

        From the Bhagavad Gita

THE WAY OF LOVE

Arjuna:
Of those who love you as the Lord of Love,
Ever present in all, and those who seek you
As the nameless, formless Reality,
Which way is sure and swift, love or knowledge?

Sri Krishna:
For those who set their hearts on me
And worship me with unfailing devotion and faith,
The way of love leads sure and swift to me.

Those who seek the transcendental Reality,
Unmanifested, without name or form,
Beyond the reach of feeling and of thought,
With their senses subdued and mind serene
And striving for the good of all beings,
They too will verily come unto me.

Yet hazardous
And slow is the path to the Unrevealed,
Difficult for physical man to tread.
But they for whom I am the goal supreme,
Who do all work renouncing self for me
And meditate on me with single-hearted devotion,
These will I swiftly rescue
From the fragment's cycle of birth and death
To fullness of eternal life in me.

Still your mind in me, still yourself in me,
And without doubt you shall be united with me,
Lord of Love, dwelling in your heart.
But if you cannot still your mind in me,
Learn to do so through the practice of meditation.
If you lack the will for such self-discipline,
Engage yourself in selfless service of all around you,
For selfless service can lead you at last to me.
If you are unable to do even this,
Surrender yourself to me in love,
Receiving success and failure with equal calmness
As granted by me.

Better indeed is knowledge than mechanical practice.
Better than knowledge is meditation.
Better still is surrender in love,
Because there follows immediate peace.

That one I love who is incapable of ill will,
And returns love for hatred.
Living beyond the reach of *I* and *mine*
And of pleasure and pain, full of mercy,
Contented, self-controlled, firm in faith,
With all their heart and all their mind given to me—
With such people I am in love.

Not agitating the world or by it agitated,
They stand above the sway of elation,
Competition, and fear, accepting life
Good and bad as it comes. They are pure,

Efficient, detached, ready to meet every demand
I make on them as a humble instrument of my work.
> *From the* Bhagavad Gita

O Sadhu! the simple union is the Best.
Since the day when I met with my Lord, there has been no
    end to the sport of our love.
I shut not my eyes, I close not my ears, I do not mortify my
    body;
I see with eyes open and smile, and behold His beauty every-
    where:
I utter His Name, and whatever I see, it reminds me of Him;
    whatever I do, it becomes His worship.
The rising and the setting are one to me; all contradictions
    are solved.
Wherever I go, I move round Him,
All I achieve is His service:
When I lie down, I lie prostrate at His feet.

He is the only adorable one to me: I have none other.
My tongue has left off impure words, it sings His glory day
    and night:
Whether I rise or sit down, I can never forget Him; for the
    rhythm of His music beats in my ears.

Kabir says: "My heart is frenzied, and I disclose in my soul
    what is hidden. I am immersed in that one great bliss
    which transcends all pleasure and pain."
> *Kabir*

O friend, understand: the body
is like the ocean,
rich with hidden treasures.

Open your inmost chamber and light its lamp.

Within the body are gardens,
rare flowers, peacocks, the inner Music;
within the body a lake of bliss,
on it the white soul-swans take their joy.

And in the body, a vast market—
go there, trade,
sell yourself for a profit you can't spend.

Mira says, her Lord is beyond praising.
Allow her to dwell near Your feet.
>   *Mirabai*

Like a silkworm weaving
her house with love
from her marrow,
     and dying
in her body's threads
winding tight, round
and round,
     I burn
desiring what the heart desires.

Cut through, O lord,
my heart's greed,
and show me
your way out,

O lord white as jasmine.

Who cares
     who strips a tree of leaf
     once the fruit is plucked?

Who cares
     who lies with the woman
     you have left?

Who cares
     who ploughs the land
     you have abandoned?

After this body has known my lord
     who cares if it feeds
     a dog
     or soaks up water?

Like an elephant
lost from his herd
suddenly captured,

remembering his mountains,
    his Vindhyas,
    I remember.

A parrot
come into a cage
remembering his mate,
    I remember.

O lord white as jasmine
show me
your ways.
    Call me: Child, come here,
    come this way.
        Mahadeviyakka

WHO CAN KEEP A BLAZING FIRE TIED IN A COTTON CLOTH?

My intimate companion,
why not plunge into union
    with the Great Goddess Kali?
Discover your spiritual anxiety
    to be without the slightest ground.

The obscure night of your religious quest is over
    and the day of truth is dawning.
The sunlight of Mother Wisdom instantly pervades
    the landscape of awareness,
for darkness is not a substance that offers resistance.
Precious Kali, you have risen as the morning sun,
opening the lotus centers of my subtle perception
    to your naked, timeless radiance.

Proliferating systems of ritual and philosophy
    attempt to throw dust into the eyes
of the eternal wisdom that abides in every soul.
How can any system transcend the play of relativity?

But when relative existence is revealed
    as the country fair of Mother's sheer delight,
there are no teachers and nothing to teach,
no students and nothing to learn.
The actors and their lines are simply expressions
    of the Wisdom Goddess
who directs this entire drama.
Be confident that you will soon awaken fully
    as the essence of her reality!

The courageous lover tastes the bliss of the Beloved
    and enters the secret city of the Goddess,
passing beyond the threshold of ecstasy
    into the open expanse of enlightenment.
Astonished by this sudden journey,
Mother's poet now sings madly:
"My delusion is gone, gone, utterly gone!
Who can obscure truth?
Who can keep a blazing fire tied in a cotton cloth?"
            Ramprasad

I WOULD NOT EVEN CARE TO BE AN EMPEROR

Mother of the Universe,
I have no desire to exercise power.
I would not even care to be an emperor.
Sweet Mother, please grant me
    two simple meals each day
and wealth enough to thatch the palm roof
    of my clean earthen house,
where I offer dreaming and waking
    as red flowers at your feet.

My green village dwelling is the abode
    of your golden radiance, O Goddess.
What need have I for more elaborate construction?
If you surround me with the complex architecture
    of stature and possession,
I will refuse to call you *Mother* ever again.

O Kali, give me just enough to serve lovingly
    whatever guests may visit me.
Plain metal plates and cups will do.
Daily existence in the heart of my extended family
    is the worship beyond worship
that perceives Mother Reality
    as every being, every situation, every breath.

I will never leave this natural way of life
    to become a stern ascetic
or a teacher honored by the world.
There is only one longing this poet's soul
    declares over and over:
"Mother! Mother! Mother!
May every moment of my existence
    merge completely with your essence."
                    Ramprasad

THE NECTAR OF SELF-AWARENESS

I honor the God and the Goddess,
The eternal parents of the universe.

The Lover, out of boundless love,
    takes the form of the Beloved.
What beauty!
Both are made of the same nectar
    and share the same food.

Out of Supreme Love
    they swallow each other up,
But separate again
    for the joy of being two.

They are not completely the same
    but neither are they different.
None can tell exactly what they are.

How intense is their longing
    to be with each other.
This is their greatest bliss.
Never, even in jest,

Do they allow their unity
   to be disturbed.

They are so averse to separation
That even though they have become
   this entire world,
Never for a moment do they let a difference
   come between them.

Even though they see
   all that is animate and inanimate,
   as arising from within themselves,
Never do they recognize a third.

They sit together
   in the same place,
Both wearing a garment of light.
From the beginning of time
   they have been together,
Reveling in their own Supreme Love.

The difference they created
   to enjoy this world
Had one glimpse of their intimacy
And could not help
   but merge back into the bliss
   found in their union.

Without the God
   there is no Goddess,
And without the Goddess
   there is no God.

How sweet is their love!   \
The entire universe
   is too small to contain them,
Yet they live happily
   in the tiniest particle. . . .

Jnanadeva says,
"I honor the union of Shiva and Shakti,
   who devour this world of name and form

like a sweet dish.
All that remains is the One."

Embracing each other
    they merge into One,
As darkness merges with the light
At the breaking of dawn.

When we discover their Unity
All words and all thoughts
    dissolve into silence,
Just as when the Universal Deluge comes,
    the waters of the ocean, and of the Ganges,
    will merge into one. . . .

A reflected image disappears
    when the mirror is removed,
Ripples merge back into the water
    when the wind becomes still.

When sleep comes to an end
    a man returns to his own senses.
Now my individuality has come to an end,
    and I have returned to Shiva and Shakti.

Salt gives up its salty taste
    to become one with the ocean;
I gave up my individual self
    and became Shiva and Shakti.

When the covering is removed,
    the air inside a plantain tree
    merges with the air outside.
And this is how I honor Shiva and Shakti—
    by removing all separation and
    becoming one with them.
                Jnaneshwar

TRUTH IS ONE

People worship God according to their tastes and temperaments.
The mother cooks the same fish differently for her children, that
each one may have what suits his stomach. For some she cooks

the rich dish of pilau. But not all the children can digest it. For those with weak stomachs she prepares soup. Some, again, like fried fish or pickled fish. It depends on one's taste. . . .

I see people who talk about religion constantly quarreling with one another. Hindus, Mussulmans, Brahmos, Saktas, Vaishnavas, Saivas all quarrel with one another. They haven't the intelligence to understand that He who is called Krishna is also Siva and the Primal Shakti, and that it is He, again, who is called Jesus and Allah. "There is only one Rama and He has a thousand names."

Truth is one; only It is called by different names. All people are seeking the same Truth; the variance is due to climate, temperament, and name. A lake has many ghats. From one ghat the Hindus take water in jars and call it *jal*. From another ghat the Mussulmans take water in leather bags and call it *pani*. From a third the Christians take the same thing and call it "water." Suppose someone says that the thing is not *jal* but *pani*, or that it is not *pani* but water, or that it is not water but *jal*. It would indeed be ridiculous. But this very thing is at the root of the friction among sects, their misunderstandings and quarrels. This is why people injure and kill one another, and shed blood, in the name of religion. But this is not good. Everyone is going toward God. They will all realize Him if they have sincerity and longing of heart.

Ramakrishna

MY JOURNEY INTO THE MOTHER

God made me pass through the disciplines of the various paths. . . .

I practiced the discipline of the Tantra under the bel-tree. At that time I could see no distinction between the sacred tulsi and any other plant. In that state I sometimes ate the leavings from a jackal's meal, food that had been exposed the whole night, part of which might have been eaten by snakes or other creatures. Yes, I ate that stuff.

Sometimes I rode on a dog and fed him with *luchi*, also eating part of the bread myself. I realized that the whole world was filled with God alone. One cannot have spiritual realization without destroying ignorance; so I would assume the attitude of a tiger and devour ignorance. . . .

I vowed to the Divine Mother that I would kill myself if I did not see God. I said to her: "O Mother, I am a fool. Please teach me what is contained in the Vedas, the Puranas, the Tantras, and the other scriptures.". . .

I had all the experiences that one should have, according to the scriptures, after one's direct perception of God. I behaved like a child, like a madman, like a ghoul, like an inert person.

I saw the visions described in the scriptures. Sometimes I saw the universe filled with sparks of fire. Sometimes I saw all the quarters glittering with light, as if the world were a lake of mercury. Sometimes I saw the world as if it were made of liquid silver. Sometimes, again, I saw all the quarters illumined as if with the light of Roman candles. So you see my experiences tally with those described in the scriptures.

It was revealed to me further that God Himself has become the universe and all its living beings and the twenty-four cosmic principles. . . .

Oh, what a state God kept me in at that time! One experience would hardly be over before another overcame me. It was like the movement of the husking-machine: no sooner is one end down than the other goes up.

I would see God in meditation, in the state of *samadhi*, and I would see the same God when my mind came back to the outer world. When looking in the mirror I would see Him alone, and when looking on the reverse side I saw the same God.

> *Ramakrishna*

THE MOTHER

The Divine Mother revealed to me in the Kali temple that it was She who had become everything. She showed me that everything was full of Consciousness. The Image was Consciousness, the altar was Consciousness, the water-vessels were Consciousness, the door-sill was Consciousness, the marble floor was Consciousness—all was Consciousness.

I found everything inside the room soaked, as it were, in Bliss—the Bliss of Satchidananda. I saw a wicked man in front of the Kali temple; but in him also I saw the Power of the Divine Mother vibrating.

That was why I fed a cat with the food that was to be offered to the Divine Mother. I clearly perceived that the Divine Mother Herself had become everything—even the cat.

Whatever we see or think about is the manifestation of the Mother, of the Primordial Energy, the Primal Consciousness. Creation, preservation, and destruction, living beings and the universe, and further, meditation and the meditator, *bhakti* [devotion] and *prema* [divine love]—all these are manifestations of the glory of that Power. . . .

Brahman, the Godhead, and Shakti, the Primal Energy, are like the snake and its wriggling motion. Thinking of the snake, one must think of its wriggling motion, and thinking of the wriggling motion, one must think of the snake. Or they are like milk and its whiteness. Thinking of milk one has to think of its color, that is, whiteness, and thinking of the whiteness of milk, one has to think of milk itself. Or they are like water and its wetness. Thinking of water, one has to think of its wetness, and thinking of the wetness of water, one has to think of water. . . .

The Primordial Power is ever at play. She is creating, preserving, and destroying in play, as it were. This power is called Kali. Kali is . . . Brahman and Brahman is . . . Kali. It is one and the same Reality. When we think of It as inactive, that is to say, not engaged in the acts of creation, preservation, and destruction, then we call it Brahman. But when It engages in these activities, then we call it Kali or Shakti. The Reality is one and the same; the difference is in name and form. . . .

A man once saw the image of the Divine Mother wearing a sacred thread. He said to the worshiper: "What? You have put the sacred thread on the Mother's neck!" The worshiper said: "Brother, I see that you have truly known the Mother. But I have not yet been able to find out whether She is male or female; that is why I have put the sacred thread on Her image."

That which is Shakti is also Brahman. That which has form, again, is without form. That which has attributes, again, has no attributes. Brahman is Shakti; Shakti is Brahman. They are not two. These are only two aspects, male and female, of the same Reality, Existence-Knowledge-Bliss Absolute.

Ramakrishna

Pray to the Divine Mother with a longing heart. Her vision
dries up all craving . . . and completely destroys all
attachment. . . . It happens instantly if you think of Her as your
own mother. She is by no means a godmother. She is your own
mother. With a yearning heart persist in your demands on Her.
The child holds to the skirt of its mother and begs a penny of
her to buy a kite. Perhaps the mother is gossiping with her
friends. At first she refuses to give the penny and says to the
child: "No, you can't have it. Your daddy has asked me not to
give you money. . . . You will get into trouble if you play with a
kite now." The child begins to cry and will not give up his demand. Then the mother says to her friends, "Excuse me a moment. Let me pacify this child." Immediately she unlocks the
cash-box with a click and throws the child a penny.

You too must force your demand on the Divine Mother. She
will come to you without fail.

> *Ramakrishna*

PERFECT AWARENESS

The *paramahamsa* [awakened being] is like a five-year-old
child. He sees everything filled with Consciousness. At one time
I was staying at Kamarpukur when Shivaram, my nephew, was
four or five years old. One day he was trying to catch grasshop-
pers near the pond. The leaves were moving. To stop their
rustling he said to the leaves: "Hush! Hush! I want to catch a
grasshopper." Another day it was stormy. It rained hard. Shivaram was with me inside the house. There were flashes of
lightning. He wanted to open the door and go out. I scolded
him and stopped him, but still he peeped out now and then.
When he saw the lightning he exclaimed, "There, uncle! They
are striking matches again!"

The *paramahamsa* is like a child. He cannot distinguish between a stranger and a relative. He isn't particular about
worldly relationships. One day Shivaram said to me, "Uncle,
are you my father's brother or his brother-in-law?". . .

Sometimes the *paramahamsa* behaves like a madman. When
I experienced that divine madness I used to worship my own

sexual organ as the Siva-phallus. But I can't do that now. A few days after the dedication of the temple at Dakshineswar, a madman came there who was really a sage endowed with the Knowledge of Brahman. He had a bamboo twig in one hand and a potted mango-plant in the other, and was wearing torn shoes. He didn't follow any social conventions. After bathing in the Ganges he didn't perform any religious rites. He ate something that he carried in a corner of his wearing-cloth. Then he entered the Kali temple and chanted hymns to the Deity. The temple trembled. . . . The madman wasn't allowed to eat at the guest-house, but he paid no attention to this slight. He searched for food in the rubbish heap where the dogs were eating crumbs from the discarded leaf-plates. Now and then he pushed the dogs aside to get his crumbs. The dogs didn't mind either. Haladhari followed him and asked: "Who are you? Are you a *purnajnani* [a perfect knower of Brahman]?" The madman whispered, "Sh! Yes, I am a *purnajnani*." Haladhari followed him a great way when he left the garden. After passing the gate he said to Haladhari: "What else shall I say to you? When you no longer make any distinction between the water of this pool and the water of the Ganges, then you will know that you have Perfect Knowledge." Saying this he walked rapidly away.

Ramakrishna

I HAVE RAISED BOTH MY HANDS

"It is a joy to merge the mind in the Indivisible Brahman through contemplation. And it is also a joy to keep the mind on the Lila, the Relative, without dissolving it in the Absolute.

"A mere *jnani* is a monotonous person. He always analyzes, saying: 'It is not this, not this. The world is like a dream.' But I have 'raised both my hands.' Therefore I accept everything.

"Listen to a story. Once a woman went to see her weaver friend. The weaver, who had been spinning different kinds of silk thread, was very happy to see her friend and said to her: 'Friend, I can't tell you how happy I am to see you. Let me get you some refreshments.' She left the room. The woman looked at the threads of different colors and was tempted. She hid a bundle of thread under one arm. The weaver returned presently with the refreshments and began to feed her guest with enthusiasm. But, looking at the thread, she realized that her friend had taken a bundle. Hitting upon a plan to get it back, she said: 'Friend, it is so long since I have seen you. This is a day of great joy for me. I feel very much like asking you to dance with me.' The friend said, 'Sister, I am feeling very happy too.' So the two friends began to dance together. When the weaver saw that her friend danced without raising her hands, she said: 'Friend, let us dance with both hands raised. This is a day of great joy.' But the guest pressed one arm to her side and danced raising only the other. The weaver said: 'How is this friend? Why should you dance with only one hand raised? Dance with me raising both hands. Look at me. See how I dance with both hands raised.' But the guest still pressed one arm to her side. She danced with the other hand raised and said with a smile, 'This is all I know of dancing.'"

The Master continued: "I don't press my arm to my side. Both my hands are free. I am not afraid of anything. I accept both the Nitya and the Lila, both the Absolute and the Relative."

Ramakrishna

THE DIVINE MOTHER

There are three ways of being of the Mother of which you can become aware when you enter into touch of oneness with the Conscious Force that upholds us and the universe. Transcendent, the original supreme Shakti, she stands above the worlds and links the creation to the ever unmanifest mystery of the Supreme. Universal, the cosmic Mahashakti, she creates all these beings and contains and enters, supports and conducts all these million processes and forces. Individual, she embodies the power of these two vaster ways of her existence, makes them living and near to us and mediates between the human personality and the divine Nature.

The one original transcendent Shakti, the Mother stands above all the worlds and bears in her eternal consciousness the Supreme Divine. Alone, she harbors the absolute Power and the ineffable Presence; containing or calling the Truths that have to be manifested, she brings them down from the Mystery in

which they were hidden into the light of her infinite consciousness and gives them a form of force in her omnipotent power
and her boundless life and a body in the universe. . . .

All is her play with the Supreme; all is her manifestation of
the mysteries of the Eternal, the miracles of the Infinite. All is
she, for all are parcel and portion of the divine Conscious-
Force. Nothing can be here or elsewhere but what she decides
and the supreme sanctions; nothing can take shape except what
she moved by the Supreme perceives and forms after casting it
into seed in her creating Ananda.

The Mahashakti, the universal Mother, works out whatever
is transmitted by her transcendent consciousness from the
Supreme and enters into the worlds that she has made; her
presence fills and supports them with the divine spirit and the
divine all-sustaining force and delight without which they could
not exist. That which we call Nature or Prakriti is only her
most outward executive aspect; she marshals and arranges the
harmony of her forces and processes, impels the operations of
Nature and moves among them secret or manifest in all that
can be seen or experienced or put into motion of life. Each of
the worlds is nothing but one play of the Mahashakti of that
system of Worlds or universe, who is there as the cosmic Soul
and Personality of the transcendent Mother. Each is something
that she has seen in her vision, gathered into her heart of
beauty and power and created in her Ananda.

Aurobindo

ALL FOR HER

If you want to be a true doer of divine works, your first aim
must be to be totally free from all desire and self-regarding ego.
All your life must be an offering and a sacrifice to the Supreme;
your only object in action shall be to serve, to receive, to fulfill,
to become a manifesting instrument of the Divine Shakti in her
works. You must grow in the divine consciousness till there is
no difference between your will and hers, no motive except her
impulsion in you, no action that is not her conscious action in
you and through you.

Until you are capable of this complete dynamic identification, you have to regard yourself as a soul and body created for

her service, one who does all for her sake. Even if the idea of the separate worker is strong in you and you feel that it is you who do the act, yet it must be done for her. All stress of egoistic choice, all hankering after personal profit, all stipulation of self-regarding desire must be extirpated from the nature. There must be no demand for fruit and no seeking for reward; the only fruit for you is the pleasure of the Divine Mother and the fulfillment of her work, your only reward a constant progression in divine consciousness and calm and strength and bliss. The joy of service and the joy of inner growth through works is the sufficient recompense of the selfless worker.

But a time will come when you will feel more and more that you are the instrument and not the worker. For first by the force of your devotion your contact with the Divine Mother will become so intimate that at all times you will have only to concentrate and to put everything into her hands to have her present guidance, her direct command or impulse, the sure indication of the thing to be done and the way to do it and the result. And afterwards you will realize that the divine Shakti not only inspires and guides, but initiates and carries out your works; all your movements are originated by her, all your powers are hers, mind, life and body are conscious and joyful instruments of her action, means for her play, molds for her manifestation in the physical universe. There can be no more happy condition than this union and dependence; for this step carries you back beyond the border-line from the life of stress and suffering in the ignorance into the truth of your spiritual being, into its deep peace and its intense Ananda.

While this transformation is being done it is more than ever necessary to keep yourself free from all taint of the perversions of the ego. Let no demand or insistence creep in to stain the purity of the self-giving and the sacrifice. There must be no attachment to the work or the result, no laying down of conditions, no claim to possess the Power that should possess you, no pride of the instrument, no vanity or arrogance. Nothing in the mind or in the vital or physical parts should be suffered to distort to its own use or seize for its own personal and separate satisfaction the greatness of the forces that are acting through you. Let your faith, your sincerity, your purity of aspiration be absolute and pervasive of all the planes and layers of the being; then every disturbing element and distorting influence will progressively fall away from your nature.

The last stage of this perfection will come when you are completely identified with the Divine Mother and feel yourself to be no longer another and separate being, instrument, servant or worker but truly a child and eternal portion of her consciousness and force. Always she will be in you and you in her; it will be your constant, simple and natural experience that all your thought and seeing and action, your very breathing or moving come from her and are hers. You will know and see and feel that you are a person and power formed by her out of herself, put out from her for the play and yet always safe in her, being of her being, consciousness of her consciousness, force of her force, Ananda of her Ananda. When this condition is entire and her supramental energies can freely move you, then you will be perfect in divine works; knowledge, will, action will become sure, simple, luminous, spontaneous, flawless, an outflow from the Supreme, a divine movement of the Eternal.

Aurobindo

THE SUPRAMENTAL FORCE

Here the evolution takes place in a material universe; the foundation, the original substance, the first established all-conditioning status of things is Matter. Mind and Life are evolved in Matter, but they are limited and modified in their action by the obligation to use its substance for their instrumentation and by their subjection to the law of material Nature even while they modify what they undergo and use. . . .

An original creative or evolutionary Power there must be: but, although Matter is the first substance, the original and ultimate Power is not an inconscient material Energy; for then life and consciousness would be absent, since Inconscience cannot evolve consciousness nor an inanimate Force evolve life. There must be, therefore, since Mind and Life also are not that, a secret Consciousness greater than Life-Consciousness or Mind-Consciousness, an Energy more essential than the material Energy. Since it is greater than Mind, it must be a supramental

Consciousness-Force; since it is a power of essential substance other than Matter, it must be the power of that which is the supreme essence and substance of all things, a power of the Spirit. There is a creative energy of Mind and a creative Life-Force, but they are instrumental and partial, not original and decisive: Mind and Life do indeed modify the material substance they inhabit and its energies and are not merely determined by them, but the extent and way of this material modification and determination are fixed by the inhabitant and all-containing Spirit through a secret indwelling light and force of Supermind, an occult gnosis—an invisible self-knowledge and all-knowledge. If there is to be an entire transformation, it can only be by the full emergence of the law of the Spirit; its power of Supermind or gnosis must have entered into Matter and it must evolve in Matter. It must change the mental into the supramental being, make the inconscient in us conscious, spiritualize our material substance, erect its law of gnostic consciousness in our whole evolutionary being and nature.

Aurobindo

THE NEW BEING

The mental man has not been Nature's last effort or highest reach—though he has been, in general, more fully evolved in his own nature than those who have achieved themselves below or aspired above him; she has pointed man to a yet higher and more difficult level, inspired him with the ideal of a spiritual living, begun the evolution in him of a spiritual being. The spiritual man is her supreme supernormal effort of human creation; for, having evolved the mental creator, thinker, sage, prophet of an ideal, the self-controlled, self-disciplined, harmonized mental being, she has tried to go higher and deeper within and call out into the front the soul and inner mind and heart, call down from above the forces of the spiritual mind and higher mind and overmind and create under their light and by their influence the spiritual sage, seer, prophet, God-lover, Yogin, gnostic, Sufi, mystic. . . .

The spiritual man is the sign of this new evolution, this new and higher endeavor of Nature. But this evolution differs from the past process of the evolutionary Energy in two respects: it is conducted by a conscious effort of the human mind, and it is not confined to a conscious progression of the surface nature, but is accompanied by an attempt to break the walls of the Ignorance and extend ourselves inward into the secret principle of our present being and outward into cosmic being as well as upward toward a higher principle. Up till now what Nature had achieved was an enlarging of the bounds of our surface Knowledge-Ignorance; what it attempted in the spiritual endeavor is to abolish the Ignorance, to go inward and discover the soul and to become united in consciousness with God and with all existence. This is the final aim of the mental stage of evolutionary Nature in man; it is the initial step toward a radical transmutation of the Ignorance into the Knowledge. The spiritual change begins by an influence of the inner being and the higher spiritual mind, an action felt and accepted on the surface; but this by itself can lead only to an illumined mental idealism or to the growth of a religious mind, a religious temperament or some devotion in the heart and piety in the conduct; . . . much has to be done, we have to live deeper within, we have to exceed our present consciousness and surpass our present status of Nature.

It is evident that if we can live thus deeper within and put out steadily the inner forces into the outer instrumentation or raise ourselves to dwell on higher and wider levels and bring their powers to bear on physical existence, not merely receive influences descending from them, which is all we can now do, there could begin a heightening of our force of conscious being so as to create a new principle of consciousness, a new range of activities, new values for all things, a widening of our consciousness and life, a taking up and transformation of the lower grades of our existence—in brief, the whole evolutionary process by which the Spirit in Nature creates a higher type of being.

Aurobindo

THE NEW RACE

A supramental or gnostic race of beings would not be a race made according to a single type, molded in a single fixed pattern;

for the law of the Supermind is unity fulfilled in diversity, and therefore there would be an infinite diversity in the manifestation of the gnostic consciousness although that consciousness would still be one in its basis, in its constitution, in its all-revealing and all-uniting order. . . . In the supramental race, in the variation of its degrees, the individuals would not be cast according to a single type of individuality; each would be different from the other, a unique formation of the Being, although one with all the rest in foundation of self and sense of oneness and in the principle of his being. . . .

The gnostic individual would be the consummation of the spiritual man; his whole way of being, thinking, living, acting would be governed by the power of a vast universal spirituality. All the trinities of the Spirit would be real to his self-awareness and realized in his inner life. All his existence would be used in oneness with the transcendent and universal Self and Spirit; all his action would originate from and obey the supreme Self and Spirit's divine governance of Nature. All life would have to him the sense of the Conscious Being, within, finding its self-expression in Nature; his life and all its thoughts, feelings, acts would be filled for him with that significance and built upon that foundation of its reality. He would feel the presence of the Divine in every center of his consciousness, in every vibration of his life-force, in every cell of his body. In all the workings of his force of Nature he would be aware of the workings of the supreme World-Mother, the Supernature; he would see his natural being as the becoming and manifestation of the power of the World-Mother. In this consciousness he would live and act in an entire transcendent freedom, a complete joy of the Spirit, an entire identity with the cosmic Self and a spontaneous sympathy with all in the universe.

Aurobindo

THE NEW BODY

The body will be turned by the power of the spiritual consciousness into a true and fit and perfectly responsive instrument of the Spirit.

This new relation of the Spirit and the body assumes—and makes possible—a free acceptance of the whole of material Nature in place of a rejection; the drawing back from her, the refusal of all identification or acceptance, which is the first normal necessity of the spiritual consciousness for its liberation, is no longer imperative. To cease to be identified with the body, to separate oneself from the body-consciousness, is a recognized and necessary step whether towards spiritual liberation or towards spiritual perfection and mastery over Nature. But, this redemption once effected, the descent of the spiritual light and force can invade and take up the body also and there can be a new liberated and sovereign acceptance of material Nature. That is possible, indeed, only if there is a changed communion of the Spirit with Matter, a control, a reversal of the present balance of interaction which allows physical Nature to veil the Spirit and affirm her own dominance. In the light of a larger knowledge Matter also can be seen to be the Brahman, a self-energy put forth by the Brahman, a form and substance of Brahman; aware of the secret consciousness within material substance, secure in this larger knowledge, the gnostic light and power can unite itself with Matter and accept it as an instrument of a spiritual manifestation. . . . The Spirit has made itself Matter in order to place itself there as an instrument for the well-being, and joy of created beings, for a self-offering of universal physical utility and service. The gnostic being, using Matter but using it without material or vital attachment or desire, will feel that he is using the Spirit in this form of itself with its consent and sanction for its own purpose. There will be in him a respect for physical things, an awareness of the occult consciousness in them, a worship of the Divine, the Brahman, in what he uses, a care for a perfect and faultless use of his divine material, for a true rhythm, ordered harmony, beauty in the life of Matter, in the utilization of Matter.

As a result of this new relation between the Spirit and the body, the gnostic evolution will effectuate the spiritualization, perfection and fulfillment of the physical being.

Aurobindo

Then shall be ended here the Law of Pain.
Earth shall be made a home of Heaven's light . . .
The superconscient beam shall touch men's eyes
And the truth-conscious world come down to earth
Invading matter with the Spirit's ray,
Awakening its silence to immortal thoughts,
Awaking the dumb heart to the living Word.
This mortal life shall house Eternity's bliss,
The body's self taste immortality.

O mind, grow full of the eternal peace:
O word, cry out the immortal litany:
Built is the golden tower, the flame-child born.

The supermind shall claim the world for Light
And thrill with love of God the enamored heart
And place Light's crown on Nature's lifted head
And found Light's reign on her unshaking base. . . .
A soul shall wake in the Inconscient's house;
The mind shall be God-vision's tabernacle,
The body intuition's instrument,
And life a channel for God's visible power. . . .

The Spirit's tops and Nature's base shall draw
Near to the secret of their separate truth
And know each other as one deity.
The Spirit shall look out through Matter's gaze
And Matter shall reveal the Spirit's face.
Then man and superman shall be at one
And all the earth become a single life.
          Aurobindo, from Savitri

4
Buddhism
The Way of Clarity

Buddhist "mysticism" begins with the Buddha's own enlightenment in Bodhgaya in about 528 B.C. When in later years the Buddha was asked who he was, he did not say he was a saint or a yogi; he said he was "awake." His answer became his title because that is what "Buddha" means: the Sanskrit root *budh* signifies both "to wake up" and "to know." "Buddha" then is the "Enlightened One" or "Awakened One."

What the Buddha "awoke into" was a state he called Nirvana. Etymologically the word means to "blow out" or "to extinguish," not in a transitive sense, but as when a fire ceases to be able to exist because it has been deprived of fuel. This can seem like a negative state and the Buddha himself, to preserve our awareness of Nirvana from all conceptual limitation, refused to characterize it except in negatives. In fact, however, Nirvana is for the Buddha and Buddhists the highest goal and final flowering of the human spirit. Its literal meaning is extinction, but what is "extinguished" is the false self, the fundamentally nonexistent "empty" ego that is the source of all craving and therefore of misery of every kind. What extinction of the false self leads to is real life beyond categories or limits—"incomprehensible, indescribable, inconceivable, unutterable." All of the many rich and complex Buddhist mystical philosophies are attempts to help the human being attain this final freedom and live in the light of its compassion.

What distinguishes the Buddhist revelation from all others is the ferocity and clarity of its analysis of human pain and human consciousness and of all the ways they block or sabotage this freedom. Humanity has never had a less sentimental teacher than the Buddha—no one has dealt more honestly with the facts of imperfection and grief in the human experience; no one was more aware of the immense responsibility involved in the solitary work that had to be done to attain awakening. The Buddha refused to posture as a god. He knew himself to be a human being like other human beings and so knew that what he had attained was available to others if they were prepared to follow the path he had taken. What the Buddha bequeathed the human race was a magnificent series of clear-cut and unsparing analyses of reality and techniques of an almost scientific precision designed to help anyone at whatever stage of understanding open further into freedom.

However, even in the earliest texts of Buddhism (most of which claim to represent the Buddha's own words) there is a negative emphasis on the body, on the senses, on relationships, and on the natural world. These are all seen as sources of *dukkha*, "imperfection," and fundamentally the highest life is seen as attainable only by those who renounce everything. This harsh ideal was considerably softened in the development of Mahayana Buddhism, which unlike original Theravada Buddhism stressed the work of compassion in the world and not solitary revelation as the goal of awakening. Nevertheless, the Buddha's vision of reality as "empty," as devoid of any inherent permanence or meaning, permeates the whole of Buddhist philosophy and practice. No one can doubt the analytical brilliance of the Buddha's mind or the vast importance of the concepts he bequeathed the world, but many people now feel that the subtle extremism inherent in the Buddha's position is unhelpful in a time when the natural world is in danger of being destroyed from lack of recognition of its divine truth and beauty.

Therefore, in my selection of Buddhist mystical texts I have concentrated on those aspects of the Buddhist revelation I believe to be most helpful and balanced in view of our contemporary catastrophe: on Buddhism's wonderful clarity about the nature of mind and its understanding of "emptiness" not merely as a vision of reality but also as a way of purifying the emotions, on the Zen vision of the miracle of so-called ordinary reality, and most important, on the great ideal that Mahayana Buddhism has developed of the bodhisattva—the being who gives up all personal awakening to return again and again into the hell of illusion, of samsara (the continuing cycle of rebirth), to help rescue and liberate all other beings.

In these great visionary truths I find active the healing and balancing powers of that sacred feminine we need to reintegrate not only into every aspect of Buddhism itself but into all the later revelations as we have inherited them.

Be a lamp into yourself! Work out your liberation with diligence!
　　The Buddha

Fill your mind with compassion!
　　The Buddha

THE FOUR NOBLE TRUTHS

Monks, what is the noble truth about suffering?

Birth is suffering, old age is suffering, death is suffering, grief, lamentation, discomfort, unhappiness and despair are suffering; to wish for something and not obtain it is suffering; briefly, the five factors of attachment are suffering.

Monks, what is the noble truth about the origin of suffering?

Just this craving, leading to rebirth, accompanied by pleasure and emotion, and finding satisfaction now here now there, namely, the craving for sense-pleasure, the craving for new life and the craving for annihilation.

Monks, what is the noble truth about the cessation of suffering?

Just the complete indifference to and cessation of that very craving, the abandoning of it, the rejection of it, the freedom from it, the aversion toward it.

Monks, what is the noble truth about the way that goes into the cessation of suffering?

Just this noble eightfold way, namely, right view, right purpose, right speech, right action, right livelihood, right effort, right mindfulness, and right concentration.
　　The Buddha

DOCTRINE OF DEPENDENT ORIGINATION
(PATICCA-SAMUPPADA)

Thus have I heard:

At one time the Bhagava was residing at the market-town of Kammasadhamma in the country of Kuru. The Venerable Ananda approached the Bhagava, made obeisance to him, and seating himself on one side, addressed the Bhagava thus:

"Venerable Sir, wonderful it is! Unprecedented it is! This doctrine of *paticca-samuppada* is not only deep and profound, it also has the signs of being deep and profound. But to my mind it seems to be evident and fathomable."

"Ananda, say not so! Ananda, say not so! This doctrine of *paticca-samuppada* is not only deep and profound, it also has the signs of being deep and profound.

"Ananda, because of lack of proper understanding and penetrative comprehension of this doctrine, (the minds of) these beings are in a state like that of a snarled skein of yarn, or that of a blighted, matted bird's nest . . . and are unable to escape the miserable, ruinous realms of existence (*apaya*), or to escape from the round of existences (*samsara*)."

"Ananda, should it be asked if there is a cause for (the occurrence of) aging and death (*jara* and *marana*), the answer has to be that there is.

"Again, if it be asked what the cause of aging and death is, the answer has to be that aging and death are due to *jati*, new existence.

"Ananda, should it be asked if there is a cause for (the occurrence of) *jati*, coming into new existence, the answer has to be that there is.

"Again, if it be asked what the cause of *jati* is, the answer has to be that *jati* is due to *bhava*, the karmic causal process.

"Ananda, should it be asked if there is a cause for (the occurrence of) *bhava*, the answer has to be that there is.

"Again, if it be asked what the cause of *bhava* is, the answer has to be that *bhava* is due to *upadana*, clinging.

"Ananda, should it be asked if there is a cause for (the arising of) *upadana*, clinging, the answer has to be that there is.

"Again, if it be asked what the cause of clinging is, the answer has to be that clinging is due to *tanha*, craving.

"Ananda, should it be asked if there is a cause for (the arising of) *tanha*, craving, the answer has to be that there is.

"Again, if it be asked what the cause of *tanha* is, the answer has to be that *tanha* is due to *vedana*, sensation.

"Ananda, should it be asked if there is a cause for (the arising of) *vedana*, sensation, the answer has to be that there is.

"Again, if it be asked what the cause of *vedana* is, the answer has to be that *vedana* is due to *phassa*, contact.

"Ananda, should it be asked if there is a cause for (the occurrence of) *phassa*, contact, the answer has to be that there is.

"Again, if it be asked what the cause of *phassa* is, the answer has to be that *phassa* is due to *namarupa*, mind-and-body.

"Ananda, should it be asked if there is a cause for (the arising of) *namarupa*, mind-and-body, the answer has to be that there is.

"Again, if it be asked what the cause of *namarupa* is, the answer has to be that *namarupa* is due to *vinnana*, (birth-linking) consciousness.

"Ananda, should it be asked if there is a cause for (the arising of) *vinnana*, (birth-linking) consciousness, the answer has to be that there is.

"Again, if it be asked what the cause of *vinnana*, (birth-linking) consciousness, is the answer has to be that *vinnana* is due to *namarupa*."

"Thus, Ananda, *namarupa* conditions the arising of *vinnana*, (birth-linking) consciousness. *Vinnana* conditions the arising of *namarupa*. *Namarupa* conditions the arising of *phassa*. *Phassa* conditions the arising of *vedana*. *Vedana* conditions the arising of *tanha*. *Tanha* conditions the arising of *upadana*. *Upadana* conditions the arising of *bhava*. *Bhava* conditions the arising of *jati*. *Jati* conditions the arising of aging, death, grief, lamentation, pain, distress, and despair. In this way occurs the arising of that entire sum total of *dukkha* (the entire aggregate of suffering, pain, affliction, imperfection, impermanence, emptiness, insubstantiality, unsatisfactoriness, which are identified with the five *khandha* aggregates)."

From the Mahanidana Sutta

Know all things to be like this:
A mirage, a cloud castle,
A dream, an apparition,
Without essence, but with qualities that can be seen.

Know all things to be like this:
As the moon in a bright sky
In some clear lake reflected,
Though to that lake the moon has never moved.

Know all things to be like this:
As an echo that derives
From music, sounds, and weeping,
Yet in that echo is no melody.

Know all things to be like this:
As a magician makes illusions
Of horses, oxen, carts, and other things,
Nothing is as it appears.
            The Buddha

Couplets

Everything has mind in the lead, has
mind in the forefront, is made by mind.
If one speaks or acts with a corrupt
mind, misery will follow, as the wheel
of a cart follows the foot of the ox.

Everything has mind in the lead, has mind in the
forefront, is made by mind. If one speaks or acts
with a pure mind, happiness will follow, like a
shadow that never leaves.

"He reviled me; he injured me; he defeated me;
he deprived me." In those who harbor such
grudges, hatred never ceases.

"He reviled me; he injured me; he defeated me;
he deprived me." In those who do not harbor such
grudges, hatred eventually ceases.

Hatreds do not ever cease in this world by hating,
but by not hating; this is an eternal truth.

The Worthy

The thoughtful exert themselves; they
do not relish attachment. Like swans
leaving a lake, they abandon one
attachment after another.

Those who have no accumulation, who eat with
perfect knowledge, whose sphere is emptiness,
signlessness, and liberation, are hard to track, like
birds in the sky.

Those whose compulsions are gone, who are not
attached to food, whose sphere is emptiness,
signlessness, and liberation, are hard to track, like
birds in the sky.

Those whose senses are tranquil, like a horse well
controlled by a charioteer, who are free from
pride and have no compulsions, are the envy of
even the gods.

For one who is docile as the earth, a pillar of good
conduct, like an unpolluted lake, there are no
more compulsive routines.

The thought is calm, the speech and action are
calm, in one who is liberated and gone to serenity
by perfect knowledge.

The Buddha, from the Dhammapada

THE NATURE OF NIRVANA

King Milinda said: "I will grant you, Nagasena, that Nirvana
is absolute ease, and that nevertheless one cannot point to its
form or shape, its duration or size, either by simile or explanation, by reason or by argument. But is there perhaps some quality of Nirvàna which it shares with other things, and which
lends itself to a metaphorical explanation?"

"Its form, O king, cannot be elucidated by similes, but its qualities can."

"How good to hear that, Nagasena! Speak then, quickly, so that I may have an explanation of even one of the aspects of Nirvana! Appease the fever of my heart! Allay it with the cool sweet breezes of your words!"

"Nirvana shares one quality with the lotus, two with water, three with medicine, ten with space, three with the wishing jewel, and five with the mountain peak. As the lotus is unstained by water, so is Nirvana unstained by all the defilements. As cool water allays feverish heat, so also Nirvana is cool and allays the fever of all the passions. Moreover, as water removes the thirst of men and beasts who are exhausted, parched, thirsty, and over-powered by heat, so also Nirvana removes the craving for sensuous enjoyments, the craving for further becoming, the craving for the cessation of becoming. As medicine protects from the torments of poison, so Nirvana from the torments of the poisonous passions. Moreover, as medicine puts an end to sickness, so Nirvana to all sufferings. Finally, Nirvana and medicine both give security. And these are the ten qualities which Nirvana shares with space. Neither is born, grows old, dies, passes away, or is reborn; both are unconquerable, cannot be stolen, are unsupported, are roads respectively for birds and Arhats to journey on, are unobstructed and infinite. Like the wishing jewel, Nirvana grants all one can desire, brings joy, and sheds light. As a mountain peak is unshakable, so is Nirvana. As a mountain peak is inaccessible, so is Nirvana inaccessible to all the passions. As no seeds can grow on a mountain peak, so the seeds of all the passions cannot grow in Nirvana. And finally, as a mountain peak is free from all desire to please or displease, so is Nirvana."

From the Questions of King Milinda

UNLIMITED FRIENDLINESS

May all beings be happy and at their ease! May they be joyous and live in safety!

All beings, whether weak or strong—omitting none—in high, middle, or low realms of existence, small or great, visible or invisible, near or far away, born or to be born—may all beings be happy and at their ease!

Let none deceive another, or despise any being in any state!
Let none by anger or ill will wish harm to another!
Even as a mother watches over and protects her child, her
only child, so with a boundless mind should one cherish all living beings, radiating friendliness over the entire world, above,
below, and all around without limit. So let everyone cultivate a
boundless good will toward the entire world, uncramped, free
from ill will or enmity.

From the Majjhima Nikaya

However innumerable sentient beings are, I vow to save
them.
However inexhaustible the defilements are, I vow to extinguish them.
However immeasurable the *dharmas* are, I vow to master
them.
However incomparable enlightenment is, I vow to attain it.

Bodhisattva vows

THE HEART OF PERFECT UNDERSTANDING

The Bodhisattva Avalokita, while moving in the deep course of
Perfect Understanding, shed light on the five *skandhas* and
found them equally empty. After this penetration, he overcame
all pain.

"Listen, Shariputra, form is emptiness, emptiness is form,
form does not differ from emptiness, emptiness does not differ
from form. The same is true with feelings, perceptions, mental
formations, and consciousness.

"Hear, Shariputra, all *dharmas* are marked with emptiness;
they are neither produced nor destroyed, neither defiled nor immaculate, neither increasing nor decreasing. Therefore, in
emptiness there is neither form, nor feeling, nor perception, nor
mental formations, nor consciousness; no eye, or ear, or nose,
or tongue, or body, or mind; no form, no sound, no smell, no
taste, no touch, no object of mind; no realms of elements (from
eyes to mind-consciousness); no interdependent origins and no
extinction of them (from ignorance to old age and death); no
suffering, no origination of suffering, no extinction of suffering,
no path; no understanding, no attainment.

"Because there is no attainment, the *bodhisattvas*, supported by the Perfection of Understanding, find no obstacles for their minds. Having no obstacles, they overcome fear, liberating themselves forever from illusion and realizing perfect Nirvana. All Buddhas in the past, present, and future, thanks to this Perfect Understanding, arrive at full, right, and universal Enlightenment.

"Therefore, one should know that Perfect Understanding is a great mantra, is the highest mantra, is the unequaled mantra, the destroyer of all suffering, the incorruptible truth. A mantra of Prajnaparamita should therefore be proclaimed. This is the mantra: *Gate gate paragate parasamgate bodhi svaha* [Gone beyond, beyond, utterly beyond]."

From the Heart Sutra

THE BODHISATTVA'S INFINITE COMPASSION

A *bodhisattva* resolves: I take upon myself the burden of all suffering, I am resolved to do so, I will endure it. I do not turn or run away, do not tremble, am not terrified, nor afraid, do not turn back or despond.

And why? At all costs I must bear the burdens of all beings, in that I do not follow my own inclinations. I have made the vow to save all beings. All beings I must set free. The whole world of living beings I must rescue, from the terrors of birth, of old age, of sickness, of death and rebirth, of all kinds of moral offense, of all states of woe, of the whole cycle of birth-and-death, of the jungle of false views, of the loss of wholesome *dharmas*, of the concomitants of ignorance—from all these terrors I must rescue all beings. . . . I walk so that the kingdom of unsurpassed cognition is built up for all beings. My endeavors do not merely aim at my own deliverance. For with the help of the boat of the thought of all-knowledge, I must rescue all these beings from the stream of Samsara, which is so difficult to cross, I must pull them back from the great precipice, I must free them from all calamities, I must ferry them across the stream of Samsara. I myself must grapple with the whole mass of suffering of all beings. To the limit of my endurance I will experience in all the states of woe, found in any world system, all the abodes of suffering. And I must not cheat all beings out of my store of merit. I am resolved to abide in each single state of woe for numberless eons; and so I will help all beings to freedom, in all the states of woe that may be found in any world system whatsoever.

From the Vajradhvaha Sutra

THE BODHISATTVA'S GREAT LOVE

Manjusri, the crown prince, addressed the Licchavi Vimalakirti: "Good sir, how should a *bodhisattva* regard all living beings?"

Vimalakirti replied, "Manjusri, a *bodhisattva* should regard all living beings as a wise man regards the reflection of the moon in water or as magicians regard men created by magic."

Manjusri then asked further, "Noble sir, if a *bodhisattva* considers all living beings in such a way, how does he generate the great love toward them?"

Vimalakirti replied, "Manjusri, when a *bodhisattva* considers all living beings in this way, he thinks: 'Just as I have realized the Dharma, so should I teach it to living beings.' Thereby, he generates the love that is truly a refuge for all living beings; the love that is peaceful because it is free of grasping; the love that is not feverish, because free of passions; . . . the love that is without conflict because free of the violence of the passions; the love that is nondual because it is involved neither with the external nor with the internal; the love that is imperturbable because totally ultimate.

"Thereby he generates the love that is firm, its high resolve unbreakable, like a diamond; the love that is pure, purified in its intrinsic nature; the love that is even, its aspirations being equal; the saint's love that has eliminated its enemy; the *bodhisattva's* love that continuously develops living beings; . . . the love that is enlightenment because it is unity of experience; the love that has no presumption because it has eliminated attachment and aversion; the love that is never exhausted because it acknowledges voidness and selflessness; the love that is morality because it improves immoral living beings; the love that is tolerance because it protects both self and others; the love that is effort because it takes responsibility for all living beings; . . . the love that is wisdom because it causes attainment at the proper time; the love that is liberative technique because it shows the way everywhere; the love that is without formality because it is pure in motivation; . . . the love that is without deceit because it is not artificial; the love that is happiness because it introduces living beings to the happiness of the Buddha. Such, Manjusri, is the great love of a *bodhisattva*."

> *Vimalakirti*

THE AWAKENING OF THE THOUGHT OF ENLIGHTENMENT (BODHICITTA)

I would be a protector for those without protection, a leader for those who journey, and a boat, a bridge, a passage for those desiring the further shore.

For all creatures, I would be a lantern for those desiring a lantern, I would be a bed for those desiring a bed, I would be a slave for those desiring a slave.

I would be for creatures a magic jewel, an inexhaustible jar, a powerful spell, an universal remedy, a wishing tree, and a cow of plenty.

As the earth and other elements are, in various ways, for the enjoyment of innumerable beings dwelling in all of space;

So may I be, in various ways, the means of sustenance for the living beings occupying space, for as long a time as all are not satisfied.

As a blind man may obtain a jewel in a heap of dust, so, somehow, this Thought of Enlightenment has arisen even within me.

This elixir has originated for the destruction of death in the world. It is the imperishable treasure which alleviates the world's poverty.

It is the uttermost medicine, the abatement of the world's disease. It is a tree of rest for the wearied world journeying on the road of being.

When crossing over hard places, it is the universal bridge for all travelers. It is the risen moon of mind (*cita*), the soothing of the world's hot passion (*klesa*).

It is a great sun dispelling the darkness of the world's ignorance. It is fresh butter, surging up from the churning of the milk of the true Dharma.

For the caravan of humanity, moving along the road of being, hungering for the enjoyment of happiness, this happiness banquet is prepared for the complete refreshening of every being who comes to it.

Shantideva

THE SUPREME MYSTERY

Whoever wishes to quickly rescue himself and another should practice the supreme mystery: the exchanging of himself and the other.

Because of an excessive attachment to "self," even the slightest fear causes fear. Who would not hate that "self," who, like an enemy, is a carrier of fear; who, desiring a defense against sickness, hunger, thirst, and the like, destroys birds, fish, animals, and stands as their antagonist; who, for the sake of profit and honor would kill even his parents; who would steal even the Three Jewels, the inheritance which he has received? . . .

What wise man would desire that "self"? Who would protect it? Who would worship it? Who would not regard it as an enemy? Who would honor it?

All of those who are in a condition of unhappiness in the world are that way because of desiring their own release. All of those who are in a condition of happiness in the world are that way from seeking the release of another.

Whatever calamities there are, and whatever sorrows and fears come to the world, they are all the result of attachment to "self." Why is that attachment mine?

Not having extinguished "self," one is not able to extinguish sorrow; just as one who has not extinguished a fire is not able to extinguish the burning.

It follows that for the sake of tranquilizing my own sorrow, and for the tranquilizing of the other's sorrow, I give myself to others and I accept others like myself.

Shantideva

EMPTINESS

In order to verify nonsubstantiality or emptiness, we must first understand exactly "what" it is that is empty. Shantideva says in the Introduction to the "Deeds of the Bodhisattva" (*Bodhicharyavatara*, Chapter 140): "If we have not, before all else, apprehended the phenomenon constructed by the mind, its nonexistence cannot be established." So we cannot realize emptiness without knowing "what" is empty and "of what" it is empty.

When thinking of a tangible object that we notice is absent, we call this absence "empty," the same way we say that space is empty. But this is not the kind of emptiness we mean when we use the term "emptiness." When we speak of "emptiness," we do not mean to say that one existing entity is empty of another existing entity. Instead, to say that phenomena are "empty" means that we have taken their inherent existence as an object to refute and that it is the absence of such substantiality that constitutes emptiness.

Nor is it that the object that is being refuted previously existed and is now eliminated. It is therefore not at all the same kind of absence as when a forest that we have crossed has burned down and no longer exists; the landscape is then "empty" of the forest. The emptiness of the inherent existence of the object is that which has never really existed at all. . . .

If an object that appears inherently real existed in accordance with its appearance, then the moment we analyze it in detail its nature should become more and more clear, little by little, as we deepen our investigation. Similarly, in daily life, if something seems true to us, the more we discuss and examine it, the clearer its meaning becomes, and if we were to look for it we would certainly find it. On the other hand, if something is false, it will become indistinct and unclear when we analyze it; eventually, having no solidity in itself, it will completely fade away.

Nagarjuna says in the *Ratnavali (Precious Garland, 52–53)*:

A form seen in the distance
Becomes clearer the closer we get to it.
If a mirage were water,
Why would it vanish when we draw near?

The farther we are from the world,
The more real it appears to us;

The nearer we draw to it, the less visible it becomes,
And, like a mirage, becomes signless.
> *The Dalai Lama*

THE SELF-LIBERATED MIND

In emptiness there is no stinginess.
Stinginess arises because of confusion.
Look undeludedly into the one who is feeling stingy.
Look and maintain that without distraction.
The stinginess is cleared and turns into emptiness.
Rest undistractedly in this empty state.
That is the total purification of stinginess.
There is no generosity higher than this.
How wonderful for the *yogin* who realizes it!

In emptiness there is no anger.
Anger arises because of confusion.
Look undeludedly into the one who is feeling angry.
Look and maintain that without distraction.
The anger is cleared and turns into emptiness.
Rest undistractedly in this empty state.
That is the total purification of anger.
There is no patience higher than this.
How wonderful for the *yogin* who realizes it!

In emptiness there is no distraction.
Distraction arises because of confusion.
Look undeludedly into the one who is feeling distracted.
The distraction is cleared and turns into emptiness.
Rest undistractedly in this empty state.
This is the total purification of distraction.
There is no concentration higher than this.
How wonderful for the *yogin* who realizes it!
> *Paltrul Rinpoche*

SIX SONGS

Do not sit at home, do not go to the forest,
But recognize mind wherever you are.

When one abides in complete and perfect enlightenment,
Where is Samsara and where is Nirvana?

"This is myself and this is another."
Be free of this bond which encompasses you about,
And your own self is thereby released.

Do not err in this matter of self and other.
Everything is Buddha without exception.
Here is that immaculate and final stage,
Where thought is pure in its true nature.

The fair tree of thought that knows no duality,
Spreads through the triple world.
It bears the flower and fruit of Compassion,
And its name is service of others.

The fair tree of the Void abounds with flowers,
Acts of compassion of many kinds,
And fruit for others appearing spontaneously,
For this joy has no actual thought of another. . . .

He who clings to the Void
And neglects Compassion,
Does not reach the highest stage.
But he who practices only Compassion
Does not gain release from toils of existence.
He, however, who is strong in practice of both,
Remains neither in Samsara nor in Nirvana.
                    Saraha

BELIEVING IN MIND

The great Way has no impediments;
It does not pick and choose.
When you abandon attachment and aversion
You see it plainly.
Make a thousandth of an inch distinction,
Heaven and earth swing apart.
If you want it to appear before your eyes,
Cherish neither *for* nor *against*.

To compare what you like with what you dislike,
That is the disease of the mind.
You pass over the hidden meaning;
Peace of mind is needlessly troubled.

It is round and perfect like vast space,
Lacks nothing, never overflows.
Only because we take and reject
Do we lose the means to know its Suchness.

Don't get tangled in outward desire
Or get caught within yourself.
Once you plant deep the longing for peace
Confusion leaves of itself.

Return to the root and find meaning;
Follow sense objects, you lose the goal.
Just one instant of inner enlightenment
Will take you far beyond the emptiness of the world. . . .
          Seng Ts'an

ONE MIND

All such dualistic concepts as "ignorant" and "Enlightened,"
"pure" and "impure," are obstructions. It is because your
minds are hindered by them that the Wheel of the Law must be
turned. Just as apes spend their time throwing things away and
picking them up again unceasingly, so it is with you and your
learning. All you need is to give up your "learning," your "ignorant" and "Enlightened," "pure" and "impure," "great" and
"little," your "attachment" and "activity." Such things are
mere conveniences. . . . I hear you have studied the *sutras* of the
twelve divisions of the Three Vehicles. They are all mere empiri-
cal concepts. Really you must give them up!

So just discard all you have acquired as being no better than
a bed spread for you when you were sick. Only when you have
abandoned all perceptions, there being nothing objective to
perceive; only when phenomena obstruct you no longer; only
when you have rid yourself of the whole gamut of dualistic
concepts of the "ignorant" and "Enlightened" category, will
you at last earn the title of Transcendental Buddha. . . .

There exists just the One Mind. Truly there are no multiplicity of forms, no Celestial Brilliance, and no Glorious Victory. . . . Since no Glorious Victory was ever won, there can be no such formal entity as a Buddha; and, since no submission ever took place, there can be no such formal entities as sentient beings. . . .

Every grain of matter, every appearance is one with Eternal and Immutable Reality! Wherever your foot may fall, you are still within the Sanctuary for Enlightenment, though it is nothing perceptible. I assure you that one who comprehends the truth of "nothing to be attained" is already seated in the sanctuary where he will gain his Enlightenment.

Huang Po

ZEN WISDOM

Ordinary Mind

Zhaozhou asked Nanquan, "What is the way?"
    Nanquan said, "Ordinary mind is the way."
    Zhaozhou asked, "Shall I try for that?"
    Nanquan said, "If you try you'll miss it."
    Zhaozhou asked, "How do I know it's the way if I don't try?"
    Nanquan said, "The way has nothing to do with knowing or not knowing. Knowing is illusion; not knowing is ignorance. If you penetrate the way of no-trying, it will be wide open—empty and vast. What need is there to affirm this or deny it?"
    Zhaozhou was suddenly enlightened upon hearing this.

From "Gateless Barrier," Case 19

The Furnace of Reality

A disciple came to his master and asked, "It is terribly hot, and how shall we escape the heat?" And at once the answer came, "Let us go down to the bottom of the furnace." So the perplexed disciple asked again, "But in the furnace how shall we escape the scorching fire?" To which he received the surprising reply, "There, no further pains will harass you."

Zen story

Mind Set Free in the Dharma-Realm

Mind set free in the Dharma-realm,
I sit at the moon-filled window
Watching the mountains with my ears,
Hearing the stream with open eyes.
Each molecule preaches perfect law,
Each moment chants true sutra:
The most fleeting thought is timeless,
A single hair's enough to stir the sea.
       Shutaku

5

Judaism
The Way of Holiness

An exciting feature of modern spiritual life is the widespread re-
discovery and reevaluation of the depth, range, and magnificence of the Jewish mystical tradition that is occurring both
within the Jewish community and within the mystical community at large. For too long the image of Yahweh as a fierce puni-
tive Father God demanding total subservience to his law has
obscured a richer and more balanced vision, also inherent in Judaism, of God's love and of human beings in relation to it. The
Jewish passion for finding traces of God's presence in history,
for seeing history as imbued with divine meaning and divine
purpose, seems less limited now that the end of human and natural history seems to be in sight and the penalties of ignoring the
divine presence in matter and in laws governing the universe
and human life appear more and more obvious.

What any reverent exploration of Jewish mysticism—both as
it exists in the Bible and in its later developments in the kabbalistic tradition—will reveal is an extraordinarily ripe and affir-
mative vision of the divine and of human life. Yahweh does have
a terrifying, judgmental side; but he is also the God of transcendent mercy and majesty. Yahweh *is* conceived as "apart" in
transcendent glory from the creation, but he is also revealed *in*
the creation and the creation is envisioned as "good" and
"blessed" because of his presence within it. And while it *is* true
that the book of Genesis in the Bible shows God as giving
human beings "dominion" over nature—a position that has had
disastrous consequences—a deeper mystical insight everywhere
present in the Jewish revelation shows God as inhabiting every
part and particle of nature and of human life within nature, potentially ennobling and sacralizing everything in them. The tendency of the Asiatic religions to depreciate the body, sexuality,

and matter are wonderfully absent in this holistic, ecstatic, and celebratory vision.

What is also invigorating in Jewish mystical thought and practice is that the passion of God for humanity is seen primarily as a demand for justice and "righteousness" in human relations, for a mirroring in *this* world and *this* life the body of the sacred laws of holiness and mercy. There are no figures in the history of the world's spiritual imagination comparable to the great Hebrew prophets Isaiah, Jeremiah, Hosea, and Elijah—human beings who risked everything to call authority to the task of securing justice for all. Polytheism and the Asiatic vision of reality as "illusion" have tended toward resignation and support of the status quo; by introducing God as an *agent* into human history, the Jews made mysticism an active power within history—a source of unending and sometimes savage critique of social oppression and injustice. This was a crucial deepening of the human understanding of the divine, and one all mystics of whatever tradition now need to claim.

What anyone plunging into a serious study of the Jewish mystics will also discover is the presence, within an overwhelmingly "masculinist" vision, of many streams of thought and action that point to the inner presence of the sacred feminine within the Jewish revelation. In the highest mystical sense, this presence is attested to by Hokmah, Wisdom, portrayed in the Old Testament as the "consort" of Yahweh and the master craftswoman of the creation who is both transcendent to it and immanent in it. Later Kabbalists developed this marvelous continuation of the ancient goddess tradition into a profound vision of what they called the Shekinah (from the verb *shakhan*, the act of dwelling), whom they characterize as the "Queen" or "Bride" of Yahweh and as, in essence, the emanation of the utterly unknowable Source in reality and the glory of God within both the creation and the individual soul. In a wider mystical sense, this presence of the sacred feminine in Judaism is found in its sense of the sacredness of human life in all of its particulars when sanctified by prayer and the observation of sacred tradition: in eating, marriage, childbearing, and holy friendship as well as in prayer, contemplation, and ritual worship.

Both the vision of God as justice and the vision of life as being potentially holy in all of its particulars seem to me to be crucial now to our human survival, for they help reempower human beings with a sense of purpose in history and a sense of the potential sacred resplendence of ordinary human life when lived consciously in and for God. In Jewish mysticism humankind is not a slave or victim, but a co-creator with the divine, through worship and holy living, of a divine life on earth. In such a vision begin great, and transforming, responsibilities.

IN THE BEGINNING

In the beginning God created the heaven and the earth.

And the Earth was without form, and void; and darkness was upon the face of the deep. And the spirit of God moved upon the face of the waters.

And God said, "Let there be light": and there was light.

And God saw the light, that it was good: and God divided the light from the darkness.

And God called the light Day, and the darkness he called Night. And the evening and the morning were the first day.

And God said, "Let there be a firmament in the midst of the waters, and let it divide the waters from the waters."

And God made the firmament, and divided the waters which were under the firmament from the waters which were above the firmament: and it was so.

And God called the firmament Heaven. And the evening and the morning were the second day.

And God said, "Let the waters under the heaven be gathered unto one place, and let the dry land appear": and it was so.

And God called the dry land Earth; and the gathering together of the waters called he Seas: and God saw that it was good.

And God said, "Let the earth bring forth grass, the herb yielding seed, and the fruit tree yielding fruit after his kind, whose seed is in itself, upon the earth": and it was so.

And the earth brought forth grass, and herb yielding seed after his kind, and the tree yielding fruit, whose seed was in itself, after his kind: and God saw that it was good.

Genesis 1:1–12

The heavens declare the glory of God: and the firmament sheweth his handiwork.

Day unto day uttereth speech, and night unto night sheweth knowledge.

There is no speech nor language, where their voice is not heard.

Their line is gone out through all the earth, and their words to the end of the world. In them hath he set a tabernacle for the sun;

Which is as a bridegroom coming out of his chamber, and rejoiceth as a strong man to run a race.

His going forth is from the end of the heaven, and his circuit unto the ends of it: and there is nothing hid from the heat thereof.

The law of the Lord is perfect, converting the soul: the testimony of the Lord is sure, making wise the simple:

The statutes of the Lord are right, rejoicing the heart: the commandment of the Lord is pure, enlightening the eyes:

The fear of the Lord is clean, enduring for ever: the judgments of the Lord are true and righteous altogether.

More to be desired are they than gold, yea, than much fine gold: sweeter also than honey and the honeycomb.

Moreover, by them is thy servant warned: and in keeping of them there is great reward.

Who can understand his errors? Cleanse thou me from secret faults.

Keep back thy servant also from presumptuous sins; let them not have dominion over me: then shall I be upright, and I shall be innocent from the great transgression.

Let the words of my mouth, and the meditation of my heart, be acceptable in thy sight, O Lord, my strength and my redeemer.

Psalm 19

The Lord is my shepherd; I shall not want.

He maketh me to lie down in green pastures: he leadeth me beside the still waters.

He restoreth my soul: he leadeth me in the paths of righteousness for his name's sake.

Yea, though I walk through the valley of the shadow of death, I will fear no evil: for thou art with me; thy rod and thy staff they comfort me.

Thou preparest a table before me in the presence of mine enemies: thou anointest my head with oil; my cup runneth over.

Surely goodness and mercy shall follow me all the days of my life; and I will dwell in the house of the Lord for ever.

Psalm 23

The earth is the Lord's, and the fullness thereof; the world, and they that dwell therein.

For he hath founded it upon the seas, and established it upon the floods.

Who shall ascend into the hill of the Lord? or who shall stand in his holy place?

He that hath clean hands, and a pure heart; who hath not lifted up his soul unto vanity, nor sworn deceitfully.

He shall receive the blessing from the Lord, and righteousness from the God of his salvation.

This is the generation of them that seek him, that seek thy face, O Jacob.

Lift up your heads, O ye gates; and be ye lift up ye everlasting doors; and the King of glory shall come in.

Who is this King of Glory? The Lord strong and mighty, the Lord mighty in battle.

Lift up your heads, O ye gates; even lift them up, ye everlasting doors; and the King of glory shall come in.

Who is this King of glory? The Lord of hosts, he is the King of glory.

Psalm 24

O give thanks unto the Lord; for he is good: for his mercy endureth for ever.

O give thanks unto the God of gods: for his mercy endureth for ever.

O give thanks to the Lord of lords: for his mercy endureth for ever.

To him who alone doeth great wonders: for his mercy endureth for ever.

To him that by wisdom made the heavens: for his mercy endureth for ever.

To him that stretched out the earth above the waters: for his mercy endureth for ever.

To him that made great lights: for his mercy endureth for ever:

The sun to rule by day: for his mercy endureth for ever:

The moon and stars to rule by night: for his mercy endureth for ever.

To him that smote Egypt in their firstborn: for his mercy endureth for ever:

And brought out Israel from among them: for his mercy endureth for ever:

With a strong hand, and with a stretched out arm: for his mercy endureth for ever.

To him which divided the Red sea into parts: for his mercy endureth for ever:

And made Israel to pass through the midst of it: for his mercy endureth for ever:

But overthrew Pharaoh and his host in the Red sea: for his mercy endureth for ever.

To him which led his people through the wilderness: for his mercy endureth for ever.

Psalm 136:1–16

WHITHER SHALL I GO FROM THY SPIRIT?

O Lord, thou hast searched me, and known me.
Thou knowest my downsitting and mine uprising,
Thou understandest my thought afar off. . . .

For there is not a word in my tongue,
But, lo, O Lord, Thou knowest it altogether.
Thou hast beset me behind and before,
and laid thine hand upon me. . . .

Whither shall I go from thy spirit?
Or whither shall I flee from thy presence?
If I ascend up into heaven, thou art there:
If I make my bed in hell, behold, thou art there.

If I take the wings of the morning,
And dwell in the uttermost parts of the sea;
Even there shall thy hand lead me,
And thy right hand shall hold me.

If I say, "Surely the darkness shall cover me;
Even the night shall be light about me."
Yea, the darkness hideth not from thee;
But the night shineth as the day:
The darkness and the light are both alike to thee . . .

How precious also are thy thoughts unto me, O God!
How great is the sum of them!
If I should count them, they are more in number than the
    sand:
When I awake, I am still with thee. . . .

Search me, O God, and know my heart:
Try me, and know my thoughts:
And see if there be any wicked way in me,
And lead me in the way everlasting.
        Psalm 139: 1-2, 4-5, 7-12, 17-18, 23-24

Rise up, my love, my fair one, and come away.
For, lo, the winter is past,
The rain is over and gone;
The flowers appear on the earth;
The time of the singing of birds is come,
And the voice of the turtle is heard in our land:
The fig tree ripeneth its figs,
And the vine puts forth its blossom,

They give forth fragrance.
Arise, my love, my fair one, and come away.
Song of Songs 2:10–13

By night on my bed
I sought him whom my soul loveth:
I sought him, but found him not.
I called him but he gave no answer.
I said, "I will rise now, and go about the city,
In the streets and in the broad ways,
I will seek him whom my soul loveth":
I sought him, but found him not.
The watchmen that go about the city found me:
To them I said, "Have you seen him whom my soul loveth?"
Scarcely had I passed them,
When I found him whom my soul loveth:
I held him, and would not let him go,
Until I had brought him into my mother's house,
And into the chamber of her that conceived me.
Song of Songs 3:1–4

I am my beloved's
And he is mine.
Come, my beloved,
let us go forth into the field;
and lodge in the villages.
Let us go up early to the vineyards;
Let us see whether the vine hath budded,
whether the grape hath opened,
And the pomegranates are in bloom;
There will I give thee my love.
The mandrakes give forth fragrance,
And at our doors are all manner of precious fruits, new and
    old,
Which I have laid up for thee, O my beloved.
Song of Songs 7:10–13

Set me as a seal upon thine heart,
as a seal upon thine arm:

For love is as strong as death,
jealousy is cruel as the grave:
Its flashes are flashes of fire,
A most vehement flame.
Many waters cannot quench love,
Neither can floods drown it:
If a man would give all the wealth of his house for love
It would be utterly scorned.

Song of Songs 8:6–7

ISAIAH'S VISION OF THE LORD

In the year that king Uzziah died I saw also the Lord sitting
upon a throne, high and lifted up, and his train filled the temple.

Above it stood the seraphims: each one had six wings; with
twain he covered his face, and with twain he covered his feet,
and with twain he did fly.

And one cried unto another, and said, "Holy, holy, holy, is
the Lord of hosts: the whole earth is full of his glory."

And the posts of the door moved at the voice of him that
cried, and the house was filled with smoke.

Then said I, "Woe is me! for I am undone; because I am a
man of unclean lips, and I dwell in the midst of a people of unclean lips: for mine eyes have seen the King: the Lord of hosts."

Then flew one of the seraphims unto me, having a live coal
in his hand, which he had taken with the tongs from off the
altar:

And he laid it upon my mouth, and said, "Lo, this hath
touched thy lips, and thine iniquity is taken away, and thy sin
purged."

Also I heard the voice of the Lord, saying, "Whom shall
I send, and who will go for us?" Then said I, "Here am I
send me."

Isaiah 6:1–8

ISAIAH'S VISION OF THE MESSIAH

And there shall come forth a rod out of the stem of Jesse, and a
Branch shall grow out of his roots:

And the spirit of the Lord shall rest upon him, the spirit of wisdom and understanding, the spirit of counsel and might, the spirit of knowledge and of the fear of the Lord;

And shall make him of quick understanding in the fear of the Lord: and he shall not judge after the sight of his eyes, neither reprove after the hearing of his ears:

But with righteousness shall he judge the poor, and reprove with equity for the meek of the earth: and he shall smite the earth with the rod of his mouth, and with the breath of his lips shall he slay the wicked.

And righteousness shall be the girdle of his loins, and faithfulness the girdle of his reins.

The wolf also shall dwell with the lamb, and the leopard shall lie down with the kid: and the calf and the young lion and the fatling together: and a little child shall lead them.

And the cow and the bear shall feed; their young ones shall lie down together: and the lion shall eat straw like the ox.

And the sucking child shall play on the hole of the asp, and the weaned child shall put his hand on the cockatrice' den.

They shall not hurt nor destroy in all my holy mountain: for the earth shall be full of the knowledge of the Lord, as the waters cover the sea.

Isaiah 11:1–9

AND A FOURTH WALKED WITH THEM

Nebuchadnezzar spake and said unto them, "Is it true, O Shadrach, Meshach, and Abednego, do not ye serve my gods, nor worship the golden image which I have set up?

"Now if ye be ready that at what time ye hear the sound of the cornet, flute, harp, sackbut, psaltery, and dulcimer, and all kinds of music, ye fall down and worship the image which I have made; well: but if ye worship not, ye shall be cast the same hour into the midst of a burning fiery furnace, and who is that God that shall deliver you out of my hands?"

Shadrach, Meshach, and Abednego answered and said to the king, "O Nebuchadnezzar, we are not careful to answer thee in this matter.

"If it be so, our God whom we serve is able to deliver us from the burning fiery furnace; and he will deliver us out of thine hand, O king.

"But if not, be it known unto thee, O king, that we will not serve thy gods, nor worship the golden image which thou hast set up."

Then was Nebuchadnezzar full of fury, and the form of his visage was changed against Shadrach, Meshach, and Abednego: therefore he spake, and commanded that they should heat the furnace one seven times more than it was wont to be heated.

And he commanded the most mighty men that were in his army to bind Shadrach, Meshach, and Abednego; and to cast them into the burning fiery furnace.

Then these men were bound in their coats, their hosen, and their hats, and their other garments, and were cast into the midst of the burning fiery furnace.

Therefore because the king's commandment was urgent, and the furnace exceeding hot, the flame of the fire slew those men that took up Shadrach, Meshach, and Abednego.

And these three men, Shadrach, Meshach, and Abednego, fell down bound into the midst of the burning fiery furnace.

Then Nebuchadnezzar the king was astonished, and rose up in haste, and spake, and said unto his counsellors, "Did not we cast three men bound into the midst of the fire?" They answered and said unto the king, "True, O king."

He answered and said, "Lo, I see four men loose, walking in the midst of the fire, and they have no hurt; and the form of the fourth is like the Son of God."

Then Nebuchadnezzar came near to the mouth of the burning fiery furnace, and spake, and said, "Shadrach, Meshach, and Abednego, ye servants of the most high God, come forth, and come hither." Then Shadrach, Meshach, and Abednego came forth of the midst of the fire.

And the princes, governors, and captains, and the king's counsellors, being gathered together, saw these men, upon whose bodies the fire had no power, nor was an hair of their head singed, neither were their coats changed, nor the smell of fire had passed on them.

Daniel 3:14–27

I came out of the mouth of the most High,
   and covered the earth as a cloud.
I dwelt in high places
   and my throne is in a cloudy pillar.
I alone encompassed the circuit of heaven,
   and walked in the bottom of the deep.
I had power over the waves of the sea, and over all the earth,
   and over every people and nation. . . .

He created me from the beginning before the world,
   and I shall never fail.
In the holy tabernacle I served before him;
   and so was I established in Zion.
Likewise in the beloved city he gave me rest,
   and in Jerusalem was my power. . . .

I was exalted like a cedar in Libanus,
   and as a cypress tree upon the mountains of Hermon.
I was exalted like a palm tree in En-gaddi,
   and as a rose plant in Jericho,
   as a fair olive tree in a pleasant field,
   and grew up as a plane tree by the water. . . .

I also came out as a brook from a river,
   and as a conduit into a garden.
I said, "I will water my best garden,
   and will water abundantly my garden bed":
   and lo, my brook became a river,
   and my river became a sea.
I will yet make doctrine to shine as the morning,
   and will send forth her light afar off.
I will yet pour out doctrine as prophecy,
   and leave it to all ages for ever.
Behold that I have not laboured for myself only,
   but for all them that seek wisdom.

Sirach 24:3–6, 9–11, 13–14, 30–34

I prayed and understanding was given me: I called upon God, and the spirit of wisdom came to me. . . .

I loved her above health and beauty, and chose to have her instead of light, for the light that cometh from her never goes out. . . .

And all such things as are either secret or manifest, them I know.

For wisdom, which is the worker of all things, taught me; for in her is an understanding spirit, holy, one only, manifold, subtle, lively, clear, undefiled, plain, not subject to hurt, loving the thing that is good, quick, which cannot be letted, ready to do good,

Kind to man, steadfast, sure, free from care, having all power, overseeing all things, and going through all understanding, pure, and most subtle, spirits.

For wisdom is more moving than any motion; she passeth and goeth through all things by reason of her pureness.

For she is the breath of the power of God, and a pure influence flowing from the glory of the Almighty: . . .

For she is the brightness of the everlasting light, the unspotted mirror of the power of God, and the image of his goodness.

And being but one, she can do all things: and remaining in herself, she maketh all things new: and in all ages entering into holy souls, she maketh them friends of God, and prophets. . . .

For she is more beautiful than the sun, and above all the order of stars: being compared with light, she is found before it. . . .

I loved her, and sought her out from my youth, I desired to make her my spouse, and I was a lover of her beauty.

Wisdom 7:7, 10, 21–27, 29; 8:2

THE WISDOM OF THE RABBIS

Everything that God,
the source and substance of all,
creates in this world
flows naturally from the essence
of God's divine nature.

Creation is not a choice
but a necessity.
It is God's nature
to unfold time and space.

Creation is the extension of God.
Creation is God encountered in time and space.
Creation is the infinite in the garb of the finite.

To attend to creation is to attend to God.
To attend to the moment is to attend to eternity.
To attend to the part is to attend to the whole.
To attend to Reality is to live constructively.

        Pirke Avot 6:2

Shemaya said:

Love work.
Constructive labor
is vital to balanced living.

Hate authority. Reality alone is true.
No matter how famous the mouth,
check the words against experience.

Do not become intimate with power.
There is nothing we can control
beyond our own doing.
Relinquish power, embrace Reality,
and do what must be done.

        Pirke Avot 1:10

Shimon ben Gamliel said:

I grew up among the Sages.
All my life I listened to their words.
Yet I have found nothing better than silence.

Study is not the goal, doing is.
Do not mistake "talk" for "action."
Pity fills no stomach.
Compassion builds no house.
Understanding is not yet justice.

Whoever multiplies words causes confusion.
The truth that can be spoken
is not the Ultimate Truth.
Ultimate Truth is wordless,
the silence within the silence.
More than the absence of speech,
More than the absence of words,
Ultimate Truth is the seamless being-in-place
that comes with attending to Reality.
> Pirke Avot 1:17

Rabban Shimon ben Gamliel said:

The world stands upon three things:

Upon truth.
Upon peace.
Upon justice.

"Speak truth each to the other, establish peace
and render honest judgment in your gates" (Zech. 8:16).
> Pirke Avot 1:18

Rabban Gamliel used to say:

Desire only that which has already been given.
Want only that which you already have.

As a river empties into the ocean,
empty yourself into Reality.
When you are emptied into Reality,
you are filled with compassion,
desiring only justice.
When you desire only justice,
the will of Reality becomes your will.
When you are filled with compassion,
there is no self to oppose another
and no other to stand against oneself.
> Pirke Avot 2:4

Rabbi Jacob used to say:

Better a single moment of awakening in this world
than eternity in the world to come.

And better a single moment of inner peace
in the world to come than eternity in this world.

Why?
A single moment of awakening in this world
is eternity in the world to come.

The inner peace of the world to come
is living in this world with full attention.

The two are one, flip sides of a coin
forever tumbling and never caught.

Pirke Avot 4:22

Ben Hei Hei said:

Effort is its own reward.

We are here to do.
And through doing to learn;
and through learning to know;
and through knowing to experience wonder;
and through wonder to attain wisdom;
and through wisdom to find simplicity;
and through simplicity to give attention;
and through attention
to see what needs to be done. . . .

Pirke Avot 5:27

THE CHAIN OF BEING

God is unified oneness—one without two, inestimable. Genuine divine existence engenders the existence of all of creation. The sublime, inner essences secretly constitute a chain linking everything from the highest to the lowest, extending from the upper pool to the edge of the universe.

There is nothing—not even the tiniest thing—that is not fastened to the links of this chain. Everything is catenated in its mystery, caught in its oneness. God is one, God's secret is one, all the worlds below and above are all mysteriously one. Divine existence is indivisible.

The entire chain is one. Down to the last link, everything is linked with everything else; so divine essence is below as well as above, in heaven and on earth. There is nothing else.

Moses de León

EIN SOF AND YOU

Each of us emerges from *Ein Sof* [The Unnameable One] and is included in it. We live through its dissemination. It is the perpetuation of existence. The fact that we sustain ourselves on vegetation and animal life does not mean that we are nourished on something outside of it. This process is like a revolving wheel, first descending, then ascending. It is all one and the same, nothing is separate from it. Though life branches out further and further, everything is joined to *Ein Sof*, included and abiding in it.

Delve into this. Flashes of intuition will come and go, and you will discover a secret here. If you are deserving, you will understand the mystery of God on your own.

Moses Cardoveros

IN THE BEGINNING

In the Beginning
When the King conceived ordaining
he engraved engravings in the luster on high.
A blinding spark flashed within the concealed of the concealed
from the mystery of the Infinite,
a cluster of vapor in formlessness, set in a ring,
not white, not black, not red, not green, no color at all.
When a band spanned, it yielded radiant colors.
Deep within the spark gushed a flow, imbuing colors below,
concealed within the concealed of the mystery of the Infinite.
The flow broke through and did not break through its aura.
It was not known at all

until, under the impact of breaking through,
one high and hidden point shone.
Beyond that point, nothing is known.
So it is called Beginning.

"The enlightened will shine like the *zohar* of the sky,
and those who make the masses righteous
will shine like the stars forever and ever."

Zohar, concealed of the concealed, struck its aura.
The aura touched and did not touch this point.
Then Beginning emanated, building itself a glorious palace.
There it sowed the seed of holiness
to give birth for the benefit of the universe.

Zohar, sowing a seed of glory
like a seed of fine purple silk.
The silkworm wraps itself within, weaving itself a palace.
This palace is its praise, a benefit to all.

With Beginning, the unknown concealed one created the
    palace,
a palace called God.
The secret is: "With Beginning, _____ created God."

Moses de León, from the Zohar

WATER, LIGHT, AND COLORS

In the beginning *Ein Sof* emanated ten *sefirot* [powers of God],
which are of its essence, united with it. It and they are entirely
one. There is no change or division in the emanator that would
justify saying it is divided into parts in the various *sefirot*. Division and change do not apply to it, only to the external *sefirot*.
   To help you conceive this, imagine water flowing through
vessels of different colors: white, red, green, and so forth. As
the water spreads through those vessels, it appears to change
into the colors of the vessels, although the water is devoid of all
color. The change in color does not affect the water itself, just
our perception of the water. So it is with the *sefirot*. They are
vessels, . . . each colored according to its function, white, red,

and green, respectively, while the light of the emanator—their essence—is the water, having no color at all. This essence does not change; it only appears to change as it flows through the vessels.

Better yet, imagine a ray of sunlight shining through a stained-glass window of ten different colors. The sunlight possesses no color at all but appears to change hue as it passes through the different colors of glass. Colored light radiates through the window. The light has not essentially changed, though so it seems to the viewer. Just so with the *sefirot*. The light that clothes itself in the vessels of the *sefirot* is the essence, like the ray of sunlight. That essence does not change color at all, neither judgment nor compassion, neither right nor left. Yet by emanating through the *sefirot*—the variegated stained glass—judgment or compassion prevails.

> Moses Cardovero

THE JOURNEY OF THE SOUL

The purpose of the soul entering this body is to display her powers and actions in this world, for she needs an instrument. By descending to this world, she increases the flow of her power to guide the human being through the world. Thereby she perfects herself above and below, attaining a higher state by being fulfilled in all dimensions. If she is not fulfilled both above and below, she is not complete.

Before descending to this world, the soul is emanated from the mystery of the highest level. While in this world, she is completed and fulfilled by this lower world. Departing this world, she is filled with the fullness of all the worlds, the world above and the world below.

At first, before descending to this world, the soul is imperfect; she is lacking something. By descending to this world, she is perfected in every dimension.

> Moses de León

There is one who sings the song of his soul, discovering in his soul everything—utter spiritual fulfillment.

There is one who sings the song of his people. Emerging from the private circle of his soul—not expansive enough, not yet tranquil—he strives for fierce heights, clinging to the entire community of Israel in tender love. Together with her, he sings her song, feels her anguish, delights in her hopes. He conceives profound insights into her past and her future, deftly probing the inwardness of her spirit with the wisdom of love.

Then there is one whose soul expands until it extends beyond the border of Israel, singing the song of humanity. In the glory of the entire human race, in the glory of the human form, his spirit spreads, aspiring to the goal of humankind, envisioning its consummation. From this spring of life, he draws all his deepest reflections, his searching, striving, and vision.

Then there is one who expands even further until he unites with all of existence, with all creatures, with all worlds, singing a song with them all.

There is one who ascends with all these songs in unison—the song of the soul, the song of the nation, the song of humanity, the song of the cosmos—resounding together, blending in harmony, circulating the sap of life, the sound of holy joy.

Abraham Isaac Kook

SEXUAL HOLINESS

Sexual union is holy and pure, when performed in the right way, at the right time, and with the right intention. Let no one think that there is anything shameful or ugly in such union. God forbid! The right kind of union is called knowing. It isn't called that for nothing. Unless it were very holy, it would not be called knowing.

This matter is not as Rabbi Moses Maimonides, of blessed memory, imagined and thought in his *Guide of the Perplexed*, where he praises Aristotle for stating that the sense of touch is shameful. God forbid! This matter is not as that Greek said; what he said smacks of subtle heresy. If that Greek scoundrel believed that the world was created with divine intention, he would not have said what he said. But we, who possess the holy Torah, believe that God created everything as divine wisdom decreed. God created nothing shameful or ugly. If sexual union is shameful, then the genitals are too. Yet God created them! How could God create something blemished, disgraceful, or deficient? After all, the Torah states: "God saw everything that he had made, and behold: very good!"

The evidence is clear. In the account of Creation we read: "The two of them were naked, the man and his wife, yet they felt no shame." Before they ate from the Tree of Knowledge, they were contemplating the pure forms, and their intention was entirely holy. To them, the genitals were like eyes or hands or other parts of the body.

When sexual union is for the sake of heaven, there is nothing as holy or pure. The union of man and woman, when it is right, is the secret of civilization. Thereby, one becomes a partner with God in the act of Creation. This is the secret meaning of the saying of the sages: "When a man unites with his wife in holiness, the divine presence is between them."

Human thought has the power to expand and ascend to its origin. Attaining the source, she is joined with the upper light from which she emanated. She and he become one. Then when thought emanates once again, all becomes a single ray: the upper light is drawn down by the power of thought. In this way the divine presence appears on earth. A bright light shines and spreads around the place where the meditator is sitting. Similarly, when a man and a woman unite, and their thought joins the beyond, that thought draws down the upper light.

You should welcome her with words that draw her heart, calm her mind, and bring her joy. Then her mind will be linked with yours, and your intention with hers. Speak with her in words that arouse desire, love, and passionate union—and in words that draw her to the awe of God.

From the Iggeret ha-Qodesh

". . . All the days I have been alive, I have yearned to see
this day!
Now my desire is crowned with success.
This day itself is crowned!
Now I want to reveal words in the presence of the Blessed
    Holy One;
all those words are adorning my head like a crown!
This day will not miss its mark like the other day,
for this whole day is mine!
I have now begun revealing words
so I will not enter shamefully into the world that is coming.
I have begun! I will speak! . . .

"I have seen that all those sparks sparkle from the High
    Spark,
Hidden of all Hidden!
All are levels of enlightenment.
In the light of each and every level
there is revealed what is revealed.
All those lights are connected:
this light to that light, that light to this light,
one shining into the other,
inseparable, one from the other.

"The light of each and every spark,
called Adornments of the king, Crowns of the King—
each one shines into, joins onto
the light within, within,
not separating without.
So all rises to one level,
all is crowned with one word;
no separating one from the other.
It and Its Name are one.

"The light that is revealed is called the Garment of the King.
The light within, within is a concealed light.
In that light dwells the Ineffable One, the Unrevealed.
All those sparks and all those lights
sparkle from the Holy Ancient One,

Concealed of all Concealed, the High Spark.
Upon reflecting,
all those lights emanating—
there is nothing but the High Spark,
hidden and unrevealed! . . . "

Rabbi Abba said:
"Before the Holy Spark finished saying 'life,'
his words subsided.
I was still writing, intending to write more
but I heard nothing.
I did not raise my head:
the light was overwhelming; I could not look.
Then I started trembling.
I heard a voice calling:
'Length of days and years of life . . . ' (Prov. 3:2).
I heard another voice:
'He asked You for life . . . ' (Ps. 21:4).

"All day long, the fire in the house did not go out.
No one reached him; no one could:
light and fire surrounded him!
All day long, I lay on the ground and wailed.
After the fire disappeared
I saw the Holy Spark, Holy of Holies, leaving the world,
enwrapped, lying on his right, his face smiling."
        Moses de León, from the Zohar

6

Ancient Greece
The Way of Beauty

To those acquainted with the Greek genius for scientific skepticism, rational inquiry, and philosophical humanism, the depth, daring, variety, and richness of the Greek mystical genius come as a marvelous surprise and reveal a far greater subtlety and religious splendor than conventional accounts of the Greek mind present.

In fact, almost every facet of the mystical imagination of humankind can be found represented in the Greek mystics, as is not surprising in a culture that was always open to the wisdom of Egypt and the East. In the great pre-Socratic philosophers such as Heraclitus and Empedocles we find masters of fearless paradox who rival the anonymous seers of the Vedas and Upanishads in their awareness of the necessity of opposites and of the unity that uses, contains, and transcends them; in Plato we have a mystic philosopher who combines the passion of a Jewish prophet for justice and dignity with the hunger of a Buddhist mystic such as Nagarjuna or Shantideva for accurate distinction; in Plotinus we discover, behind transparent veils of exalted language, a lover of God as lost in rapture at the divine as the great Islamic mystics Ibn Arabi or Attar; in Marcus Aurelius we are amazed to encounter a sense of the mysterious organic wholeness of nature that could spring, in its freshness and wonder, directly from the pages of an early Taoist text. And in the Greeks' worship of their many goddesses—from Gaia to Aphrodite to Athena to Demeter—and in the complex, many-layered symbolism and ritual of the Eleusinian mysteries we are graced with almost as suggestive and polyphonic a vision of the sacred feminine as we find in the myths and mystical texts of India.

There is one strand that joins together such superficially diverse approaches: an abiding sense of the splendor and holiness of the world and of the opportunities for illumination in it. The "Hymn to Gaia" celebrates the full life as lived when the "Queen of Earth" is honored; the mystery of Eleusis is essentially a mystery of the birth of a new kind of being here on earth, a human being able to live in divine joy because awareness of the Mother sustains him or her always; behind all of Heraclitus's sometimes darkly cryptic paradoxes shines a sense of the grandeur and playfulness of the divine and the secret magnificence of human life ("Immortals are mortals, . . . living their death, dying their life"); Plato's vision of ideal truth seems to depreciate reality and the myths and illusions of ordinary life, but as the extracts from the *Timaeus* clearly demonstrate, Plato's ultimate awareness is of the "blessedness" of a world everywhere permeated by soul; in Plotinus, one of the world's supreme and highly original mystics, we find a revelation of an universe everywhere radiant with the presence of divine beauty, a beauty that waits only for the soul to be purified to reveal itself in all its wounding, ecstatic loveliness.

As well as sharing a sense of the inherent beauty of life and the world, all the Greek mystics also share what can only be called an effortless confidence in their right to know and embody that beauty. They all speak with direct authority and a desire to communicate as clearly and pungently as possible their perceptions. In the end the Greek genius for praxis and for mystical speculation reveal themselves as two halves of the same brave and complex mind, dedicated not merely to speculation on the laws of reality but to their transformatory enactment within it. Marcus Aurelius sums up this "practical" mysticism in his gruff and electric command "Waste no more time talking about great souls and how they should be. Become one yourself!"

HYMN TO GAIA

Gaia
mother of all
foundation of all
the oldest one

I shall sing to Earth

She feeds everything
that is in the world

Whoever you are
whether you live upon her sacred ground
or whether you live along the paths of the sea
you that fly

it is she who nourishes you
from her treasure-store

Queen of Earth
through you

beautiful children
beautiful harvests
come

The giving of life
and the taking of life

both are yours

Happy is the man you honor
the one who has this
has everything

His fields thicken with ripe corn
his cattle grow heavy in the pastures
his house brims over with good things

These are the men who are masters of their city
the laws are just, the women are fair
happiness and fortune richly follow them

Their sons delight
in the ecstasy of youth

Their daughters play
they dance among the flowers
skipping in and out

they dance on the grass
over soft flowers

Holy goddess, you
honored them
ever-flowing spirit

Farewell
mother of the gods
bride of Heaven
sparkling with stars

For my son, life
allow me
loved of the heart

Now
and in my other songs
I shall remember you

THE ELEUSINIAN MYSTERIES: TO DIE IS TO BE INITIATED

The initiation seems to have taken place in three stages: the
Dromena, the things done; the *Legomena*, the things said; the
Deiknymena, the things shown. There followed a special ceremony known as the *Epopteia,* the state of "having seen," only
for those initiated the previous year.

In the *Dromena* the initiates participated in a sacred pageant
that reenacted the story of Demeter and Persephone, living
through the feelings of sorrow, rage and rejoicing, probably
carrying torches in the darkness to the sound of music and
singing. Clement of Alexandria writes that "Demeter and Kore
have come to be the subject of a mystic drama, and Eleusis celebrates with torches the abduction of the daughter and the sor-
rowful wanderings of the mother." Foucart believed that the
Mystai also experienced a journey to the underworld through
wandering in the dark in the lower part of the *Telesterion*, and
that the initiates suffered the terrors of death as a condition of
initiation. . . .

There was a cave—a temple of Hades—which signified the
entrance to the underworld, and probably also an omphalos
there. Plutarch writes that "to die is to be initiated," which
though a play on words (*teleutan=teleisthai*) has the force of
tradition behind it. Only after this did the light return, and it is
more than likely that now the *Mystes* passed upward to a vision of the joyous meadows of the Elysian Fields, lit by a brilliant light. . . .

The *Legomena* consisted of short ritual invocations, more like comments accompanying the pageant and explaining the significance of the drama. The *Deiknymena*, the showing of the sacred objects, culminated in the revelation by the hierophant, which was forbidden to be told. The *Epopteia* also contained the showing of *hiera*, though we do not know what these sacred objects were.

Imagine the great hall of mysteries shrouded in darkness, thronged with people, waiting in stillness. Dim figures of priests move in the darkness, carrying torches. In the center of the darkness some secret drama is being performed. Suddenly a gong sounds like thunder, the underworld breaks open, and out of the depths of the earth Kore appears. A radiant light fills the chamber, the huge fire blazes upwards, and the hierophant chants: "The great goddess has borne a sacred child: Brimo has borne Brimos." Then, in the profound silence, he holds up a single ear of corn.

Now is the time for celebrations. There is singing and dancing in the courtyard, a great bull is sacrificed, and all the people break their fast together. Finally, the priest fills two vessels and, lifting one to the west and the other to the east, he pours the contents of the vessels on to the ground. The people, looking up to heaven, cry "Rain!" and, looking down to earth, cry "Conceive!": *hye, kye*. So end the Mysteries at Eleusis.

"Thrice-blessed are those mortals who have seen these rites and thus enter into Hades: for them alone there is life, for the others all is misery." So Sophocles writes, following the idea in the hymn, and Pindar also says, "Blessed is he who has seen this and thus goes beneath the earth; he knows the end of life, he knows the beginning given by Zeus."

> From Anne Baring and Jules Cashford,
> The Myth of the Goddess

HERACLITUS: ETERNITY IS A CHILD AT PLAY

Heraclitus says that the Universe is divisible and indivisible, generated and ungenerated, mortal and immortal, Word and Eternity, Father and Son, God and Justice.

Listening not to me but to the account, it is wise to agree that all things are one, says Heraclitus. That everyone is ignorant of this and does not agree he states as follows: *They do not comprehend how, in differing, it agrees with itself—a backward-turning connection, like that of a bow and a lyre. . . .*

That the universe is a child and an eternal king of all things for all eternity he states as follows: *Eternity is a child at play, playing draughts: the kingdom is a child's.*

That the father of everything that has come about is generated and ungenerated, creature and creator, we hear him saying: *War is father of all, king of all: some it shows as gods, some as men; some it makes slaves, some free. . . .*

That God is unapparent, unseen, unknown to men, he says in these words: *Unapparent connection is better than apparent*—he praises and admires the unknown and unseen part of his power above the known part.

Hippolytus, from Refutation of All Heresies

HERACLITUS: THE PATH UP AND DOWN IS ONE AND THE SAME

Heraclitus says that dark and light, bad and good, are not different but one and the same. For example, he reproaches Hesiod for not knowing day and night—for day and night, he says, are one, expressing it thus: *A teacher of most is Hesiod: they are sure he knows most who did not recognize day and night—for they are one. . . .*

And straight and twisted, he says, are the same: *The path of the carding-combs,* he says, *is straight and crooked* (the movement of the instrument called the screw-press in a fuller's shop is straight and crooked, for it travels upwards and in a circle at the same time)—he says it is one and the same.

And up and down are one and the same: *The path up and down is one and the same.*

And he says that the polluted and the pure are one and the same, and that the drinkable and the undrinkable are one and the same: *The sea,* he says, *is most pure and most polluted water: for fish, drinkable and life-preserving; for men, undrinkable and death-dealing.*

And he explicitly says that the immortal is mortal and the mortal immortal in the following words: *Immortals are mortals, mortals immortals: living their death, dying their life. . . .*

And he says that a judgment of the world and of everything in it comes about through fire; for *fire,* he says, *will come and judge and convict all things.*

He says that this fire is intelligent and the cause of the management of the universe, expressing it thus: *The thunderbolt steers all things* (i.e., directs everything)—by "the thunderbolt" he means the eternal fire, and he calls it need and satiety (the establishment of the world according to him being need and the conflagration satiety).

Hippolytus, from Refutation of All Heresies

HERACLITUS: CONCORDANT DISCORDANT

Surely nature longs for the opposites and effects her harmony from them. . . . That was also said by Heraclitus the Obscure: *Combinations—wholes and not wholes, concurring differing, concordant discordant, from all things one and from one all things.*

In this way the structure of the universe—I mean, of the heavens and the earth and the whole world—was arranged by one harmony through the blending of the most opposite principles.

Aristotle, On the World *396b7–8, 20–25*

LOVE AND STRIFE: A TWO-FOLD STORY

I will tell a two-fold story.
At one time they grew to be one alone from being many,
and at another they grew apart again to be many from
    being one.
Double is the generation of mortal things, double their pass-
    ing away:
one is born and destroyed by the congregation of everything,
the other is nurtured and flies apart as they grow apart
    again.
And these never cease their continual change,

now coming together by Love all into one,
now again all being carried apart by the hatred of Strife.
Thus insofar as they have learned to become one from many,
and again become many as the one grows apart,
to that extent they come into being and have no lasting life;
but insofar as they never cease their continual change,
to that extent they exist forever, unmoving in a circle.
But come, hear my word; for learning enlarges the mind.
As I said before when I revealed the limits of my words,
I will tell a two-fold story.
At one time they grew to be one alone from being many,
and at another they grew apart again to be many from
    being one—
fire and water and earth and the endless height of air,
and cursed Strife apart from them, balanced in every way,
and Love among them, equal in length and breadth.
Her you must regard with your mind: do not sit staring with
    your eyes.
She is thought to be innate also in the limbs of mortals,
by whom they think thoughts of love and perform deeds of
    union,
calling her Joy by name and Aphrodite,
whom no one has seen whirling among them—
no mortal man. Listen to the course of my argument, which
    does not deceive:
these are all equal and of the same age,
but they hold different offices and each has its own char-
    acter;
and in turn they come to power as time revolves.
And in addition to them nothing comes into being or ceases.
For if they were continually being destroyed they would no
    longer exist.
And what could increase this universe? and whence might it
    come?
And where indeed might it perish, since nothing is empty of
    them?
But these themselves exist, and passing through one another
they become different at different times—and are ever and
    always the same.
    Empedocles

In reality, the greatest blessings come by way of madness, indeed madness that is heaven-sent. It was when they were mad that the prophetess at Delphi and the priestesses at Dodona achieved so much for which both states and individuals in Greece are thankful; when sane they did little or nothing. As for the Sibyl and others who by the power of inspired prophecy have so often foretold the future to so many, and guided them aright, I need not dwell on what is obvious to everyone. Yet it is in place to appeal to the fact that madness was accounted no shame nor disgrace by the men of old who gave things their names; otherwise they would not have connected that greatest of arts, whereby the future is discerned, with this very word "madness," and named it accordingly. No, it was because they held madness to be a valuable gift, when due to divine dispensation, that they named that art as they did, though the men of today, having no sense of values, have put in an extra letter, making it not *manic* but *mantic*. . . . You see then what this ancient evidence attests. Corresponding to the superior perfection and value of the prophecy of inspiration over that of omen reading, both in name and in fact, is the superiority of heaven-sent madness over man-made sanity.

And in the second place, when grievous maladies and afflictions have beset certain families by reason of some ancient sin, madness has appeared among them, and breaking into prophecy has secured relief by finding the means thereto, namely by recourse to prayer and worship, and in consequence thereof rites and means of purification were established, and the sufferer was brought out of danger, alike for the present and for the future. Thus did madness secure, for him that was maddened aright and possessed, deliverance from his troubles.

There is a third form of possession or madness, of which the Muses are the source. This seizes a tender, virgin soul and stimulates it to rapt passionate expression, especially in lyric poetry, glorifying the countless mighty deeds of ancient times for the instruction of posterity. But if any man come to the gates of poetry without the madness of the Muses, persuaded that skill alone will make him a good poet, then shall he and his works of sanity with him be brought to nought by the poetry of madness, and behold, their place is nowhere to be found.

Such then is the tale, though I have not told it fully, of the achievements wrought by madness that comes from the gods. So let us have no fears simply on that score; let us not be disturbed by an argument that seeks to scare us into preferring the friendship of the sane to that of the passionate. For there is something more that it must prove if it is to carry the day, namely that love is not a thing sent from heaven for the advantage both of lover and beloved. What we have to prove is the opposite, namely that this sort of madness is a gift of the gods, fraught with the highest bliss. And our proof assuredly will prevail with the wise, though not with the learned.

Plato, from the Phaedrus

THE SOUL AS CHARIOTEER

Each soul is divided into three parts, two being like steeds and the third like a charioteer. . . . Now of the steeds, so we declare, one is good and the other is not, but we have not described the excellence of the one nor the badness of the other, and that is what must now be done. He that is on the more honorable side is upright and clean-limbed, carrying his neck high, with something of a hooked nose; in color he is white, with black eyes; a lover of glory, but with temperance and modesty; one that consorts with genuine renown, and needs no whip, being driven by the word of command alone. The other is crooked of frame, a massive jumble of a creature, with thick short neck, snub nose, black skin, and gray eyes; hot-blooded, consorting with wantonness and vainglory; shaggy of ear, deaf, and hard to control with whip and goad.

Now when the driver beholds the person of the beloved, and causes a sensation of warmth to suffuse the whole soul, he begins to experience a tickling or pricking of desire, and the obedient steed, constrained now as always by modesty, refrains from leaping upon the beloved. But his fellow, heeding no more the driver's goad or whip, leaps and dashes on, sorely troubling his companion and his driver, and forcing them to approach the loved one and remind him of the delights of love's commerce. For a while they struggle, indignant that he should force them to a monstrous and forbidden act, but at last, finding no end to their evil plight, they yield and agree to do his bidding. And so he draws them on, and now they are quite close and behold the spectacle of the beloved flashing upon them.

At that sight the driver's memory goes back to that form of beauty, and he sees her once again enthroned by the side of temperance upon her holy seat; then in awe and reverence he falls upon his back, and therewith is compelled to pull the reins so violently that he brings both steeds down on their haunches, the good one willing and unresistant, but the wanton sore against his will. Now that they are a little way off, the good horse in shame and horror drenches the whole soul with sweat, while the other, contriving to recover his wind after the pain of the bit and his fall, bursts into angry abuse, railing at the charioteer and his yokefellow as cowardly, treacherous deserters. Once again he tries to force them to advance, and when they beg him to delay awhile he grudgingly consents.

But when the time appointed is come, and they feign to have forgotten, he reminds them of it—struggling and neighing and pulling until he compels them a second time to approach the beloved and renew their offer—and when they have come close, with head down and tail stretched out he takes the bit between his teeth and shamelessly plunges on. But the driver, with resentment even stronger than before, like a racer recoiling from the starting rope, jerks back the bit in the mouth of the wanton horse with an even stronger pull, bespatters his railing tongue and his jaws with blood, and forcing him down on legs and haunches delivers him over to anguish.

And so it happens time and again, until the evil steed casts off his wantonness; humbled in the end, he obeys the counsel of his driver, and when he sees the fair beloved is like to die of fear. Wherefore at long last the soul of the lover follows after the beloved with reverence and awe.

Plato, from the Phaedrus

Diotima: "Well now, my dear Socrates, I have no doubt that even you might be initiated into these, the more elementary mysteries of Love. But I don't know whether you could apprehend the final revelation, for so far, you know, we are only at the bottom of the true scale of perfection.

"Never mind," Diotima went on, "I will do all I can to help you understand, and you must strain every nerve to follow what I'm saying.

"Well then," she began, "the candidate for this initiation cannot, if his efforts are to be rewarded, begin too early to devote himself to the beauties of the body. First of all, if his preceptor instructs him as he should, he will fall in love with the beauty of one individual body, so that his passion may give life to noble discourse. Next he must consider how nearly related the beauty of any one body is to the beauty of any other, when he will see that if he is to devote himself to loveliness of form it will be absurd to deny that the beauty of each and every body is the same. Having reached this point, he must set himself to be the lover of every lovely body, and bring his passion for the one into due proportion by deeming it of little or of no importance.

"Next he must grasp that the beauties of the body are as nothing to the beauties of the soul, so that wherever he meets with spiritual loveliness, even in the husk of an unlovely body, he will find it beautiful enough to fall in love with and to cherish—and beautiful enough to quicken in his heart a longing for such discourse as tends toward the building of a noble nature. And from this he will be led to contemplate the beauty of laws and institutions. And when he discovers how nearly every kind of beauty is akin to every other, he will conclude that the beauty of the body is not, after all, of so great moment.

"And next, his attention should be diverted from institutions to the sciences, so that he may know the beauty of every kind of knowledge. And thus, by scanning beauty's wide horizon, he will be saved from a slavish and illiberal devotion to the individual loveliness of a single boy, a single man, or a single institution. And, turning his eyes toward the open sea of beauty, he will find in such contemplation the seed of the most fruitful discourse and the loftiest thought, and reap a golden harvest of philosophy, until, confirmed and strengthened, he will come upon one single form of knowledge, the knowledge of the beauty I am about to speak of.

"And here," she said, "you must follow me as closely as you can.

"Whoever has been initiated so far in the mysteries of Love and has viewed all these aspects of the beautiful in due succession is at last drawing near the final revelation. And now, Socrates, there bursts upon him that wondrous vision which is the very soul of the beauty he has toiled so long for. It is an everlasting loveliness which neither comes nor goes, which neither flowers nor fades, for such beauty is the same on every hand, the same then as now, here as there, this way as that way, the same to every worshiper as it is to every other.

"Nor will his vision of the beautiful take the form of a face, or of hands, or of anything that is of the flesh. It will be neither words, nor knowledge, nor a something that exists in something else, such as a living creature, or the earth, or the heavens, or anything that is—but subsisting of itself and by itself in an eternal oneness, while every lovely thing partakes of it in such sort that, however much the parts may wax and wane, it will be neither more nor less, but still the same inviolable whole.

"And so, when his prescribed devotion to boyish beauties has carried our candidate so far that the universal beauty dawns upon his inward sight, he is almost within reach of the final revelation. And this is the way, the only way, he must approach, or be led toward, the sanctuary of Love.

"Starting from individual beauties, the quest for the universal beauty must find him ever mounting the heavenly ladder, stepping from rung to rung—that is, from one to two, and from two to *every* lovely body, from bodily beauty to the beauty of institutions, from institutions to learning, and from learning in general to the special lore that pertains to nothing but the beautiful itself—until at last he comes to know what beauty is. . . .

"And remember," she said, "that it is only when he discerns beauty itself through what makes it visible that a man will be quickened with the true, and not the seeming, virtue or it is virtue's self that quickens him, not virtue's semblance. And when he has brought forth and reared this perfect virtue, he shall be called the friend of god, and if ever it is given to man to put on immortality, it shall be given to him."

Plato, from the Symposium

SOCRATES ON ILLUSION AND REALITY: THE CAVE

"Picture men dwelling in a sort of subterranean cavern with a long entrance open to the light on its entire width. Conceive them as having their legs and necks fettered from childhood, so that they remain in the same spot, able to look forward only, and prevented by the fetters from turning their heads. Picture further the light from a fire burning higher up and at a distance behind them, and between the fire and the prisoners and above them a road along which a low wall has been built, as the exhibitors of puppet shows have partitions before the men themselves, above which they show the puppets."

"All that I see," he said.

"See also, then, men carrying past the wall implements of all kinds that rise above the wall, and human images and shapes of animals as well, wrought in stone and wood and every material, some of these bearers presumably speaking and others silent."

"A strange image you speak of," he said, "and strange prisoners."

"Like to us," I said. "For, to begin with, tell me do you think that these men would have seen anything of themselves or of one another except the shadows cast from the fire on the wall of the cave that fronted them?"

"How could they," he said, "if they were compelled to hold their heads unmoved through life?"

"And again, would not the same be true of the objects carried past them?"

"Surely."

"If then they were able to talk to one another, do you not think that they would suppose that in naming the things that they saw they were naming the passing objects?"

"Necessarily."

"And if their prison had an echo from the wall opposite them, when one of the passers-by uttered a sound, do you think that they would suppose anything else than the passing shadow to be the speaker?"

"By Zeus, I do not," said he.

"Then in every way such prisoners would deem reality to be nothing else than the shadows of the artificial objects."

"Quite inevitably," he said.

"Consider, then, what would be the manner of the release and healing from these bonds and this folly if in the course of nature something of this sort should happen to them. When one was freed from his fetters and compelled to stand up suddenly and turn his head around and walk and to lift up his eyes to the light, and in doing all this felt pain and, because of the dazzle and glitter of the light, was unable to discern the objects whose shadows he formerly saw, what do you suppose would be his answer if someone told him that what he had seen before was all a cheat and an illusion, but that now, being nearer to reality and turned toward more real things, he saw more truly? And if also one should point out to him each of the passing objects and constrain him by questions to say what it is, do you not think that he would be at a loss and that he would regard what he formerly saw as more real than the things now pointed out to him?"

"Far more real," he said.

"And if he were compelled to look at the light itself, would not that pain his eyes, and would he not turn away and flee to those things which he is able to discern and regard them as in very deed more clear and exact than the objects pointed out?"

"It is so," he said.

"And if," said I, "someone should drag him thence by force up the ascent which is rough and steep, and not let him go before he had drawn him out into the light of the sun, do you not think that he would find it painful to be haled along, and would chafe at it, and when he came out into the light, that his eyes would be filled with its beams so that he would not be able to see even one of the things that we call real?"

"Why, no, not immediately," he said.

"Then there would be need of habituation, I take it, to enable him to see the things higher up. And at first he would most easily discern the shadows and, after that, the likenesses or reflections in water of men and other things, and later, the things themselves, and from there he would go on to contemplate the appearances in the heavens and heaven itself, more easily by night, looking at the light of the stars and the moon, than by day the sun and the sun's light."

"Of course."

"And so, finally, I suppose, he would be able to look upon the sun itself and see its true nature, not by reflections in water or phantasms of it in an alien setting, but in and by itself in its own place."

"Necessarily," he said.

"And at this point he would infer and conclude that this it is that provides the seasons and the courses of the year and presides over all things in the visible region, and is in some sort the cause of all these things that they have seen."

"Obviously," he said, "that would be the next step."

"Well then, if he recalled to mind his first habituation and what passed for wisdom there, and his fellow bondsmen, do you not think that he would count himself happy in the change and pity them?"

"He would indeed."

"And if there had been honors and commendations among them which they bestowed on one another and prizes for the man who is quickest to make out the shadows as they pass and best able to remember their customary precedences, sequences, and coexistences, and so most successful in guessing at what was to come, do you think he would be very keen about such rewards, and that he would envy and emulate those who were honored by these prisoners and lorded it among them, or that he would feel with Homer and greatly prefer while living on earth to be serf of another, a landless man, and endure anything rather than opine with them and live that life?"

"Yes," he said, "I think that he would choose to endure anything rather than such a life."

"And consider this also," said I. "If such a one should go down again and take his old place would he not get his eyes full of darkness, thus suddenly coming out of the sunlight."

"He would indeed."

"Now if he should be required to contend with these perpetual prisoners in 'evaluating' these shadows while his vision was still dim and before his eyes were accustomed to the dark—and

this time required for habituation would not be very short—
would he not provoke laughter, and would it not be said of him
that he had returned from his journey aloft with his eyes ruined
and that it was not worthwhile even to attempt the ascent? And
if it were possible to lay hands on and even to kill the man who
tried to release them and lead them up, would they not kill him?"

"They certainly would," he said.

"This image then, dear Glaucon, we must apply as a whole
to all that has been said, likening the region revealed through
sight to the habitation of the prison, and the light of the fire in
it to the power of the sun. And if you assume that the ascent
and the contemplation of the things above is the soul's ascen-
sion to the intelligible region, you will not miss my surmise,
since that is what you desire to hear. But God knows whether it
is true.

"But, at any rate, my dream as it appears to me is that in the
region of the known the last thing to be seen and hardly seen is
the idea of good, and that when seen it must needs point us to
the conclusion that this is indeed the cause for all things of all
that is right and beautiful, giving birth in the visible world to
light, and the author of light and itself in the intelligible world
being the authentic source of truth and reason, and that anyone
who is to act wisely in private or public must have caught sight
of this. . . .

"It is the duty of us, the founders of the Republic, then,"
said I, "to compel the best natures to attain the knowledge
which we pronounced the greatest and to win to the vision of
the good, to scale that ascent, and when they have reached the
heights and taken an adequate view, we must not allow what is
now permitted."

"What is that?"

"That they should linger there," I said, "and refuse to go
down again among those bondsmen and share their labors and
honors, whether they are of less or of greater worth."

"Do you mean to say that we must do them this wrong, and
compel them to live an inferior life when the better is in their
power?"

"You have again forgotten, my friend," said I, "that the law
is not concerned with the special happiness of any class in the
state, but is trying to produce this condition in the city as a

whole, harmonizing and adapting the citizens to one another by persuasion and compulsion, and requiring them to impart to one another any benefit which they are severally able to bestow upon the community, and that in itself creates such men in the state, not that it may allow each to take what course pleases him, but with a view to using them for the binding together of the commonwealth."

"True," he said, "I did forget it."

"Observe, then, Glaucon," said I, "that we shall not be wronging, either, the philosophers who arise among us, but that we can justify our action when we constrain them to take charge of the other citizens and be their guardians. . . . You have received a better and more complete education than the others, and you are more capable of sharing both ways of life. Down you must go then, each in his turn, to the habitation of the others and accustom yourselves to the observation of the obscure things there. For once habituated you will discern them infinitely better than the dwellers there, and you will know what each of the 'idols' is and whereof it is a semblance, because you have seen the reality of the beautiful, the just and the good. So our city will be governed by us and you with waking minds, and not, as most cities now which are inhabited and ruled darkly as in a dream by men who fight one another for shadows and wrangle for office as if that were a great good, when the truth is that the city in which those who are to rule are least eager to hold office must needs be best administered and most free from dissension, and the state that gets the contrary type of ruler will be the opposite of this."

Plato, from the Republic

A VISION OF THE CREATION

This question we must ask about the world. Which of the patterns had the artificer in view when he made it—the pattern of the unchangeable or of that which is created? If the world be indeed fair and the artificer good, it is manifest that he must have looked to that which is eternal, but if what cannot be said without blasphemy is true, then to the created pattern. Everyone will see that he must have looked to the eternal, for the world is the fairest of creations and he is the best of causes. . . .

Let me tell you then why the creator made this world of generation. He was good, and the good can never have any jealousy of anything. And being free from jealousy, he desired that all things should be as like himself as they could be. This is in the truest sense the origin of creation and of the world, as we shall do well in believing on the testimony of wise men. God desired that all things should be good and nothing bad, so far as this was attainable. Wherefore also finding the whole visible sphere not at rest, but moving in an irregular and disorderly fashion, out of disorder he brought order, considering that this was in every way better than the other. Now the deeds of the best could never be or have been other than the fairest, and the creator, reflecting on the things which are by nature visible, found that no unintelligent creature taken as a whole could ever be fairer than the intelligent taken as a whole and again that intelligence could not be present in anything which was devoid of soul. For which reason, when he was framing the universe, he put intelligence in soul, and soul in body, that he might be the creator of a work which was by nature fairest and best. On this wise, using the language of probability, we may say that the world came into being—a living creature truly endowed with soul and intelligence by the providence of God. . . .

Such was the whole plan of the eternal God about the god that was to be; he made it smooth and even, having a surface in every direction equidistant from the center, a body entire and perfect, and formed out of perfect bodies. And in the center he put the soul, which he diffused throughout the body, making it also to be the exterior environment of it, and he made the universe a circle moving in a circle, one and solitary, yet by reason of its excellence able to converse with itself, and needing no other friendship or acquaintance. Having these purposes in view he created the world a blessed god.

Plato, from the Timaeus

THIS UNIVERSE

It would be unsound to condemn this universe as less than beautiful, or as less than the noblest universe possible on the corporeal level. A majestic organism complete within itself, the minutest part related to the whole, a marvelous artistry shown not only in the stateliest parts but in those of such littleness you would not have thought Providence would bother about them ... the exquisite design of fruits and leaves, the abundance and the delicacy and diversity of flowers. ...

The Divine Intellect, then, in Its unperturbed serenity has brought the universe into being by communicating from Its own store to matter; and this emanation of the Divine Intellect is Reason [or *Logos*]. This Logos within a seed contains all the parts and qualities concentrated in identity; there is no distinction, no internal hindering; then there comes a pushing into bulk, part rises in distinction from part, and at once the members of the organism stand in each other's way and begin to wear each other down. Yet while each utters its own voice, all is brought into an ordered system by the ruling Reason.

Plotinus, from the Enneads

THE PRINCIPLE AND BEAUTY

Let us go back to the source, and indicate at once the Principle that bestows beauty on material things.

Undoubtedly this Principle exists; it is something that is perceived at the first glance, something which the Soul names as from an ancient knowledge and, recognizing, welcomes it, enters into unison with it.

But let the Soul fall in with the Ugly and at once it shrinks within itself, denies the thing, turns away from it, not accordant, resenting it.

Our interpretation is that the Soul—by the very truth of its nature, by its affiliation to the noblest Existents in the hierarchy of Being—when it sees anything of that kin, or any trace of that kinship, thrills with an immediate delight, takes its own to itself, and thus stirs anew to the sense of its nature and of all its affinity.

But, is there any such likeness between the loveliness of this world and the splendors in the Supreme? Such a likeness in the particulars would make the two orders alike: but what is there in common between beauty here and beauty There?

We hold that all the loveliness of this world comes by communion in Ideal-Form.

All shapelessness whose kind admits of pattern and form, as long as it remains outside of Reason and Idea, is ugly by that very isolation from the Divine-Thought. And this is the Absolute Ugly: an ugly thing is something that has not been entirely mastered by pattern, that is by Reason, the Matter not yielding at all points and in all respects to Ideal-Form.

But where the Ideal-Form has entered, it has grouped and coordinated what from a diversity of parts was to become a unity: it has rallied confusion into cooperation: it has made the sum one harmonious coherence: for the Idea is a unity and what it molds must come to unity as far as multiplicity may.

And on what has thus been compacted to unity, Beauty enthrones itself, given itself to the parts as to the sun: when it lights on some natural unity, a thing of like parts, then it gives itself to that whole. Thus, for an illustration, there is the beauty, conferred by craftsmanship, of all a house with all its parts, and the beauty which some natural quality may give to a single stone.

This, then, is how the material thing becomes beautiful—by communicating in the thought (Reason, Logos) that flows from the Divine.

Plotinus, from the Enneads

THE SOUL AND BEAUTY

And the Soul includes a faculty peculiarly addressed to Beauty—one incomparably sure in the appreciation of its own, when Soul entire is enlisted to support its judgment.

Or perhaps the Soul itself acts immediately, affirming the Beautiful where it finds something accordant with the Ideal-Form within itself, using this Idea as a canon of accuracy in its decision.

But what accordance is there between the material and that which antedates all Matter?

On what principle does the architect, when he finds the house standing before him correspondent with his inner ideal of a house, pronounce it beautiful? Is it not that the house before him, the stones apart, is the inner idea stamped upon the mass of exterior matter, the indivisible exhibited in diversity?

So with the perceptive faculty: discerning in certain objects the Ideal-Form which has bound and controlled shapeless matter, opposed in nature to Idea, seeing further stamped upon the common shapes some shape excellent above the common, it gathers into unity what still remains fragmentary, catches it up and carries it within, no longer a thing of parts, and presents it to the Ideal-Principle as something concordant and congenial, a natural friend: the joy here is like that of a good man who discerns in a youth the early signs of a virtue consonant with the achieved perfection within his own soul. . . .

But there are earlier and loftier beauties than these. In the sense-bound life we are no longer granted to know them, but the Soul, taking no help from the organs, sees and proclaims them. To the vision of these we must mount, leaving sense to its own low place.

As it is not for those to speak of the material world who have never seen them or known their grace—men born blind, let us suppose—in the same way those must be silent upon the beauty of noble conduct and of learning and all that order who have never cared for such things, nor may those tell of the splendor of virtue who have never known the face of Justice and of Moral-Wisdom beautiful beyond the beauty of Evening and of Dawn.

Such vision is for those only who see with the Soul's sight—and at the vision, they will rejoice, and awe will fall upon them and a trouble deeper than all the rest could ever stir, for now they are moving in the realm of Truth.

This is the spirit that Beauty must ever induce, wonderment and a delicious trouble, longing and love and a trembling that is all delight. For the unseen all this may be felt as for the seen; and this the Souls feel for it, every Soul in some degree, but those the more deeply that are the more truly apt to this higher love—just as all take delight in the beauty of the body but all are not stung as sharply, and those only that feel the keener wound are known as Lovers.

Plotinus, from the Enneads

THE GLORY OF THIS WORLD

Do not suppose that a man becomes good by despising the world and all the beauties that are in it. They [the Gnostics] have no right to profess respect for the gods of the world above. When we love a person, we love all that belongs to him; we extend to the children the affection we feel for the parent. Now every Soul is a daughter of the Godhead. How can *this world* be separated from the *spiritual* world? Those who despise what is so nearly akin to the spiritual world prove that they know nothing of the spiritual world, except in name.

Let it [any individual soul] make itself worthy to contemplate the Great Soul by ridding itself, through quiet recollection, of deceit and of all that bewitches vulgar souls. For it let all be quiet; let all its environment be at peace. Let the earth be quiet and the sea and air, and the heaven itself waiting. Let it observe how the Soul flows in from all sides into the resting world, pours itself into it, penetrates it and illumines it. Even as the bright beams of the sun enlighten a dark cloud and give it a golden border, so the Soul when it enters into the body of the heaven gives it life and timeless beauty and awakens it from sleep. So the world, grounded in a timeless movement by the Soul which suffuses it with intelligence, becomes a living and blessed being.

The Soul gives itself to every point in this vast body, and vouchsafes its being to every part, great and small, though these parts are divided in space and manner of disposition, and though some are opposed to each other, others dependent on each other. But the Soul is not divided, nor does it split up in order to give life to each individual. All things live by the Soul *in its entirety*; it is all present everywhere. The heaven, vast and various as it is, is one by the power of the Soul, and by it is this universe of ours Divine. The sun too is Divine, and so are the stars; and we ourselves, if we are worth anything, are so on account of the Soul.

Plotinus, from the Enneads

CUT AWAY EVERYTHING

But what can it be which is loftier than that existence—a life compact of wisdom, untouched by struggle and error, or than this Intellect which holds the Universe with all there is of life and intellect?

If we answer "The Making Principle," there comes the question, "making by what virtue"? And unless we can indicate something higher there than in the made, our reasoning has made no advance; we rest where we were.

We must go higher—if it were only for the reason that the self-sufficiency of the Intellectual-Principle is that of a totality of which each member is patently indigent, and that each has participated in The One and, as drawing on unity, is itself not unity.

What then is this in which each particular entity participates, the author of being to the universe and to each item of the total?

Since it is the author of all that exists, and since the multiplicity in each thing is converted into a self-sufficing existence by this presence of The One, so that even the particular itself becomes self-sufficing, then clearly this principle, author at once of Being and of self-sufficingness, is not itself a Being but is above Being and above even self-sufficing.

May we stop, content, with that? No: the Soul is yet, and even more, in pain. Is she ripe, perhaps, to bring forth, now that in her pangs she has come so close to what she seeks? No: we must call upon yet another spell if anywhere the assuagement is to be found. Perhaps in what has already been uttered, there lies the charm if only we tell it over often? No: we need a new, further incantation. All our effort may well skim over every truth, and through all the verities in which we have part, and yet the reality escapes us when we hope to affirm, to understand: for the understanding, in order to its affirmation, must possess itself of item after item; only so does it traverse all the field: but how can there be any such peregrination of that in which there is no variety?

All the need is met by a contact purely intellective. At the moment of touch there is no power whatever to make any affirmation; there is no leisure; reasoning upon the vision is for afterwards. We may know we have had the vision when the Soul has suddenly taken light. This light is from the Supreme and is the Supreme; we may believe in the Presence when He comes bringing light: the light is the proof of the advent. Thus, the Soul unlit remains without that vision; lit, it possesses what it sought. And this is the true end set before the Soul, to take that light, to see the Supreme by the Supreme and not be the light of any other principle—to see the Supreme which is also the means to the vision; for that which illumines the Soul is that which it is to see, just as it is by the sun's own light that we see the sun.

But how is this to be accomplished?

Cut away everything.

Plotinus, from the Enneads

HONOR THE HIGHEST

Honor the highest thing in the Universe; it is the power on which all things depend; it is the light by which all of life is guided. Honor the highest within yourself; for it too is the power on which all things depend, and the light by which all life is guided.

Dig within. Within is the wellspring of Good; and it is always ready to bubble up, if you just dig.

You have seen a hand, a foot, or perhaps a head severed from its body and lying some distance away. Such is the state a man brings himself to—as far as he is able—when he refuses to accept what befalls him, breaks away from helping others, or pursues self-seeking action. You become an outcast from the unity of Nature; though born of it, your own hand has cut you from it. Yet here is the beautiful proviso: it lies within your own power to join Nature once again. God has not granted such a favor to any other part of creation: to return again, after having been separated and cleft asunder.

O Universe, all that is in tune with you is also in tune with me! Every note of your harmony resonates in my innermost being. For me nothing is early and nothing is late, if it is timely for you. O Nature, all that your seasons bring is fruit for me. From thee come all things; in thee do all things live and grow; and to thee do all things return. . . .

Waste no more time talking about great souls and how they should be. Become one yourself!

Marcus Aurelius, from Meditations

7

∾

Islam
The Way of Passion

"Islam" is derived from the Arabic root *s-l-m,* which means "peace" and, secondarily, "surrender." A helpful translation of "Islam" might then be "that peace that comes when one's entire being and life are surrendered to God." It is the truth of this peace-in-surrender to the one omnipotent and all-merciful God that Muhammad, the founder-prophet of Islam, proclaims in the Qur'an.

Muhammad was illiterate and received the Qur'an—a glorious poetic and religious masterpiece—in a series of almost annihilating revelations; the whole book, Muhammad's entire revelation to humankind of the One God, blazes with awe and wonder at the power and glory of Allah. More than any other of the great religious books of humankind, the Qur'an, both in its structure and its metaphorical language, dedicates itself to transmitting a living sense of God's both beautiful and terrible grandeur, a grandeur forever beyond any human being's ability to understand or imitate.

From the extent and depth of Muhammad's experience of this grandeur of Allah, the One God, arose that quality of passionate, loving humility that characterizes his life and mission and also the very best of Islamic mysticism: Muhammad never confused himself with the Godhead, whose majesty had often nearly destroyed him, and never claimed to be anything but God's messenger; his bearing and behavior were characterized by the most exquisite courtesy of soul and reverence toward all life.

Muhammad's God of unnameable grandeur was also a God of the most intimate, mysterious love; in his "surrender" to the dictates and demands of that love Muhammad set the tone, by his wonder at God's power and his concern for justice, not only for the civilization and ritual and legal practices that were to grow from his great revelation but also for the mysticism that was to be engendered from it.

Islamic mysticism is, to a very great extent, Sufism. Sufism is notoriously difficult to define, but in essence it is a path of the heart, of the sacred heart, a path of direct experience through abandon to God of the living presence of Allah the Beloved. The Sufis have always enjoyed a rather ambiguous relationship with Islamic orthodoxy and in modern times have been severely persecuted, but the Sufi revelation of God's glory and intimacy and of what the greatest Sufi poet of all, Rumi, called the Fire of Love has never enjoyed a more thrilling response than it does now. For many modern mystics, the Sufi poets in general and Rumi in particular offer the most compelling witness imaginable to the ordeals and magnificence of the mystical life.

Why is this? Most of all, I think, it is because of the passion of the Sufi approach to reality—a passion that embraces, as Muhammad did, the whole of reality as a manifestation of the divine and that seeks to burn out in the Flame of Love. This passion comes to know the whole of reality as "burning" in the Fire of the Presence, as utterly consumed and sanctified by love, and finds the meaning of human existence in the living out as deeply and fully as possible of ecstatic joy, and service of all beings in the name of God. Every conceivable human emotion—rage, sadness, pleading, longing—is fed into and transformed by this overwhelming passion that answers and echoes mysteriously the passion in the heart of God himself. In the life and work of Rumi, who combines the mystic awareness of a Buddha or Christ with the intellect of a Plato and the literary genius of a Shakespeare, we have not only the most complete representative of the Sufi vision but one of the supreme mystics of humankind.

The Sufi poets and philosophers in general and Rumi in particular offer the modern seeker an extraordinarily vivid witness to the rigor and splendor of the complete mystical life and to the immense force of love it can release into reality. It is this witness to the force of love active in reality that makes them crucial to the revolution of the sacred feminine that is attempting to take place now in our contemporary disaster. The clue to the transformation of the sacred feminine lies in cultivating that power of adoration of the Beloved that the Sufis cultivated with such brave and wild perfection and in the revelation of the total sa-

credness of reality that it brings. The path of the sacred feminine
is in essence the path of the sacred heart, and the witness of the
great Sufi poets and "lovers" to the terrors, raptures, and revelations of this path is of inestimable value.

"O My servants who believe!
Surely My earth is vast,
Therefore Me alone should you serve."
> *Qur'an*

In the name of God, the Compassionate, the Merciful

All praise belongs to God,
Lord of all worlds,

the Compassionate, the Merciful,

Ruler of Judgment Day.

It is You that we worship,
and to You we appeal for help.

Show us the straight way,

the way of those You have graced,
not of those on whom is Your wrath,
nor of those who wander astray.
> *Qur'an, Surah 1, "The Opening"*

To God belong the East and the West;
and wherever you turn,
there is the Face of God.

For God is omnipresent, all-knowing . . .
God is the originator
of the heavens and the earth;
and whenever God decrees anything
God says to it, "Be!"
and it is. . . .

And your God is one God
there is no God but The One,
the Compassionate,
the Merciful.

Behold, in the creation
of the heavens and the earth,
and the alternation of night and day,
and the ships that sail on the sea
to profit the people,
and the water God rains from the skies,
thereby enlivening the earth
after it has died,
and spreading animals of all kinds
thereupon,
and in the shifting of the winds
and the clouds
enslaved between the heavens and the earth:
therein are signs
for a discerning people.
From the Qur'an, Surah 2

For with God are the keys of the unseen;
no one knows them
but God.
And God knows
what is on the land
and in the sea;
and not a single leaf falls
but God knows it.
And there is not a single grain
in the darknesses of earth,
nor anything green, or withered,
but is in an open Book. . . .
From the Qur'an, Surah 6

When your Lord brought forth
from the offspring of Adam
descendants from their loins
and had them testify
regarding themselves
—"Am I not your Lord?"—
They said, "Oh yes! We so testify!"

Lest you say on Judgment Day,
"We were heedless of this!"
           From the Qur'an, Surah 7

In the name of God, the Compassionate, the Merciful

God is the light
of the heavens and the earth.
The simile of God's light
is like a niche in which is a lamp,
the lamp in a globe of glass,
the globe of glass as if it were a shining star,
lit from a blessed olive tree
neither of the East nor of the West,
its light nearly luminous even if fire did not touch it.
Light upon light!
God guides to this light
whomever God will:
and God gives people examples;
and God knows all things.

The light is in houses
which God has allowed to be raised
that the name of God be remembered there,
where God is glorified
in the mornings and the evenings,

by people who are not diverted
by business or commerce
from remembrance of God
and persistence in prayer
and giving of alms,
as they fear a day on which
hearts and eyes will be transformed,
that God may reward them
for the best of what they did,
and grant them even more
from the grace divine.
And God provides without measure
to whomever God will. . . .

And among the signs of God
is creating you all from dust;
and there you are, humankind,
propagating widely.
And among the signs of God
is having created for you
mates from yourselves
that you may feel at home with them,
and God put love and kindness among you.
Surely in that is a sign
for a reflective people.
And among the signs of God
is the creation of the heavens and the earth
and the diversity of your languages and your complexions.
Surely in that is a sign for the knowing. . . .
            From the Qur'an, Surah 24, "Light"

And among the signs of God
is showing you lightning,
occasion for fear and for hope;
and God sends water
down from the sky,
enlivening the earth
after it has died.
Surely in that is a sign
for an intelligent people.
And among the signs of God
is that sky and earth stand by divine decree.
Then when God calls you
with a call from earth,
you will all come forth.
To God belongs everyone
in the heavens and the earth:
all are obedient to God.
            From the Qur'an, Surah 30

"I was a hidden treasure and I wanted to be known: That is why I created the world."

"I cannot fit into my heavens or into my earth but I fit into the heart of my believing servant."

"He who knows himself knows his Lord."

"My slave does not cease to draw near to me with devotion of her own free will until I love her. And when I love her, I am the hearing with which she hears, the sight with which she sees, . . . the foot she walks on."

"Paradise is at the feet of the Mothers."

"The heart of the believer is the place of the revelation of God. The heart of the believer is the throne of God. The heart of the believer is the mirror of God."

ACCORDING TO ABU DHARR-AL-GHIFARI, THE PROPHET
SAID, REPORTING THE WORDS OF HIS LORD:

O my servants, I have forbidden myself injustice, and have declared it forbidden among you: so do not be unjust one to another.

O my servants, each of you is lost except the one I guide: so ask me, and I will guide you.

O my servants, each of you is hungry, except the one whom I feed: so ask me, and I will feed you.

O my servants, each of you is naked, except the one I clothe: so ask me, and I will clothe you.

O my servants, you commit faults night and day; I am the forgiver of sins: so ask forgiveness from me, and I will forgive you.

O my servants, it is in vain that you try to harm me or bring me profit. If all of you—each human being and each angel—had the heart of the purest being among you, that would add nothing to my kingdom. And if all of you—from the first to the last—had the heart of the most perverted being among you, that would take nothing away from my kingdom. And if all of you, angels and men, from the first to the last, stayed in one

place to invoke me and I satisfied the demand of each of you,
that would not diminish anything I possess—it would be like a
needle penetrating the sea.

Hadiths, *An-Nanawi Collection*

Kill me, O my trustworthy friends,
For in my being killed is my life.

Love is that you remain standing
In front of your Beloved.
When you are deprived of all your attributes,
Then His attributes become your qualities.

Between me and You, there is only me.
Take away the me, so only You remain.

I am the Supreme Reality.
Al-Hallaj

O Lord, whatever share of this world
You could give to me,
Give it to your enemies:
Whatever share of the next world
You want to give to me—
Give it to your friends.
You are enough for me.

O God, my whole concern and desire in this world,
Is that I should always remember you
Above all the things of this world,
And that in the next
I should meet with you alone.
That is why I always pray: "Your will be done."

O my Lord,
if I worship you
from fear of hell, burn me in hell.

If I worship you
from hope of Paradise, bar me from its gates.

But if I worship you
for yourself alone, grant me then the beauty of your Face.
Rabi'a

My heart has become capable of every form:
   It is a pasture for gazelles
And a monastery for Christian monks,
   And a temple for idols,
   And the pilgrim's Ka'ba,
   And the tablets of the Torah,
   And the Book of the Koran.
   I follow the religion of Love:
Whatever way love's camel takes,
That is my religion, my faith.
     Ibn Arabi

THE WISDOM OF DIVINITY IN THE WORD OF ADAM

The Reality wanted to see the essences of His Most Beautiful Names or, to put it another way, to see His own Essence, in an all-inclusive object encompassing the whole [divine] Command, which, qualified by existence, would reveal to Him His own mystery. For the seeing of a thing, itself by itself, is not the same as its seeing itself in another, as it were in a mirror; . . .

The Reality gave existence to the whole Cosmos [at first] as an undifferentiated thing without anything of the spirit in it, so that it was like an unpolished mirror. It is in the nature of the divine determination that He does not set out a location except to receive a divine spirit, which is also called [in the Qur'an] *the breathing into him*. The latter is nothing other than the coming into operation of the undifferentiated form's [innate] disposition to receive the inexhaustible overflowing of Self-revelation, which has always been and will ever be. . . .

For the Reality, he is as the pupil is for the eye through which the act of seeing takes place. Thus he is called *insan* [meaning both man and pupil], for it is by him that the Reality looks on His creation and bestows the Mercy [of existence] on them. He is Man, the transient [in his form], the eternal [in his essence]; he is the perpetual, the everlasting, the [at once] discriminating and unifying Word.

It is by his existence that the Cosmos subsists and he is, in relation to the Cosmos, as the seal is to the ring, the seal being that place whereon is engraved the token with which the King seals his treasure. So he is called the Vice-Regent, for by him God preserves His creation, as the seal preserves the king's treasure. So long as the king's seal is on it no one dares to open it except by his permission, the seal being [as it were] a regent in charge of the kingdom. Even so is the Cosmos preserved so long as the Perfect Man remains in it.

> *Ibn Arabi*

EIGHTEEN THOUSAND UNIVERSES THROUGH EIGHTEEN THOUSAND EYES

It is essential to know that as there is no end to the Ipseity of God or to His qualification, consequently the Universes have no end or number, because the Universes are the places of manifestation for the Names and Qualities. As that which manifests is endless, so the places of manifestation must be endless. Consequently, the Qur'anic sentence: "He is at every moment in a different configuration," means equally that there is no end to the revelation of God.

The Power (*qudra*) of God is constantly and permanently in a state of Perfection. Because of this Perfection He does not reveal Himself twice to the same person in the same manner. He is constantly in new revelations, . . . so the same revelation may not ever happen to two different people.

In a *hadith* it is said: "God has eighteen thousand universes and this your world is just one universe from among them." The saying that God has eighteen thousand universes in part, and in total eighteen universes, is drawn from the *hadith* mentioned above even though there is no extremity to the revelation of God and no end to the places of the revelation of God. . . .

Hazreti 'Ali has said it this way:

> *"You thought yourself a part, small;*
> *Whereas in you there is a universe, the greatest."*

That is to say, you think of yourself as a small thing, whereas in you there is hidden the biggest of the universes. . . .

You may imagine the greatness of the Perfect Man in this manner: if eighteen thousand universes were put in a mortar and pestled to a paste, its composition would be the Perfect Man. This Man will see the eighteen thousand universes through eighteen thousand eyes. He sees each universe with the eye of senses, matters of intellect with the eye of intellect, the meanings with the eye of the heart. . . .

The meaning of the Qur'anic verse becomes clear to the gnostic: "Whichever way you turn, there is the face of God." That is to say, which ever way you turn your face, there you will find a road which leads to God. It is true that according to the rule that: "He is at every moment in a different configuration," there are states and degrees; but He shows in every wink a caprice, and in every caprice a scent, and in every scent a beauty, and in every beauty a love, and in every love a wink, and in every wink a caprice, and in every caprice a scent, and in every scent a kind of recommencement. . . .

    Ibn Arabi

FANA: ANNIHILATION

If that God who is One and All-Conquering, reveals Himself to one of His servants with the quality of the Destroyer that servant would see everything annihilated. Then, "Everything is in annihilation except His face." "Everything on earth will be annihilated and there will only remain the face of your Lord who is both Majestic and Generous." So according to these it is necessary to die today, before death. This death must come about by resolution and he in whom this state of death appears will see the complete annihilation of everything except God and will not exist himself. This non-existence is total non-existence. This is the state of annihilation in God (*fana' fi-l llah*). There, nothing is left but the Beauty of God. . . .

The man of knowledge in these affairs is lost and buried in nothingness. While this is so, God grants him an existence from His own existence and paints him with the Divine Color. All the qualities inside him and outside him are changed. That day the earth becomes another earth, equally the skies. . . .

Then God gives this man of knowledge a Divine sight, ear, tongue . . . and starts him in questions and answers; this way the servant has passed through non-existence, and having reached the Universe of Existence, he becomes existent by the existence of God. His real understanding and knowledge starts after this.

Ibn Arabi

THE HOOPOE'S CALL TO THE BIRDS TO SET OUT TO FIND THE SIMORGH

How long will you persist in blasphemy?
Escape your self-hood's vicious tyranny—
Whoever can evade the Self transcends
This world and as a lover he ascends.
Set free your soul; impatient of delay
Step out along our sovereign's royal Way:
We have a king; beyond Kaf's mountain peak
The Simorgh lives, the sovereign whom you seek,
And He is always near to us, though we
Live far from His transcendent majesty.
A hundred thousand veils of dark and light
Withdraw His presence from our mortal sight,
And in both worlds no being shares the throne
That marks the Simorgh's power and His alone—
He reigns in undisturbed omnipotence,
Bathed in the light of His magnificence—
No mind, no intellect can penetrate
The mystery of His unending state:
How many countless hundred thousands pray
For patience and true knowledge of the Way
That leads to Him whom reason cannot claim,
Nor mortal purity describe or name.
There soul and mind bewildered miss the mark
And, faced by Him, like dazzled eyes, are dark—
No sage could understand His perfect grace,
Nor seer discern the beauty of His face.
His creatures strive to find a path to Him,
Deluded by each new, deceitful whim,

But fancy cannot work as she would wish;
You cannot weigh the moon like so much fish!
How many search for Him whose heads are sent
Like polo-balls in some great tournament
From side to giddy side—how many cries,
How many countless groans assail the skies!
Do not imagine that the Way is short;
Vast seas and deserts lie before His court.
Consider carefully before you start;
The journey asks of you a lion's heart.
The road is long, the sea is deep—one flies
First buffeted by joy and then by sighs;
If you desire this quest, give up your soul
And make our sovereign's court your only goal.
First wash your hands of life if you would say:
"I am a pilgrim of our sovereign's Way";
Renounce your soul for love; He you pursue
Will sacrifice His inmost soul for you.
It was in China, late one moonless night,
The Simorgh first appeared to mortal sight—
He let a feather float down through the air,
And rumors of its fame spread everywhere;
Throughout the world men separately conceived
An image of its shape, and all believed
Their private fantasies uniquely true! . . .
If this same feather had not floated down,
The world would not be filled with His renown—
It is a sign of Him, and in each heart
There lies this feather's hidden counterpart.
But since no words suffice, what use are mine
To represent or to describe this sign?
Whoever wishes to explore the Way,
Let him set out—what more is there to say?'

THE END OF THE JOURNEY

Of all the army that set out, how few
Survived the Way; of that great retinue
A handful lived until the voyage was done—
Of every thousand there remained but one.

Of many who set out no trace was found.
Some deep within the ocean's depths were drowned;
Some died on mountaintops; some died of heat;
Some flew too near the sun in their conceit,
Their hearts on fire with love—too late they learned
Their folly when their wings and feathers burned;
Some met their death between the lion's claws,
And some were ripped to death by monsters' jaws;
Some died of thirst; some hunger sent insane,
Till suicide released them from their pain;
Some became weak and could no longer fly
(They faltered, fainted, and were left to die);
Some paused bewildered and then turned aside
To gaze at marvels as if stupefied;
Some looked for pleasure's path and soon confessed
They saw no purpose in the pilgrim's quest;
Not one in every thousand souls arrived—
In every hundred thousand one survived.

The Birds Arrive and Are Greeted by a Herald

A world of birds set out, and there remained
But thirty when the promised goal was gained,
Thirty exhausted, wretched, broken things,
With hopeless hearts and tattered, trailing wings,
Who saw that nameless Glory which the mind
Acknowledges as ever-undefined,
Whose solitary flame each moment turns
A hundred worlds to nothingness and burns
With power a hundred thousand times more bright
Than sun and stars and every natural light.
The awe-struck group, bewildered and amazed,
Like insubstantial, trembling atoms, gazed
And chimed: "How can we live or prosper here,
Where if the sun came it would disappear?
Our hearts were torn from all we loved; we bore
The perils of a path unknown before;
And all for this? It was not this reward
That we expected from our longed-for Lord."

It seemed their throats were cut, as if they bled
And weakly whimpered until left for dead,
Waiting for splendor to annihilate
Their insubstantial, transitory state.
Time passed; then from the highest court there flew
A herald of the starry retinue,
Who saw the thirty birds, trembling, afraid,
Their bodies broken and their feathers frayed,
And said, "What city are you from? What race?
What business brings you to this distant place?
What are your names? You seem destroyed by fear;
What made you leave your homes and travel here?
What were you in the world? What use are you?
What can such weak and clumsy creatures do?"
The group replied: "We flew here for one thing,
To claim the Simorgh as our rightful king;
We come as suppliants and we have sought
Through grievous paths the threshold of His court—
How long the Way was to complete our vow;
Of thousands we are only thirty now!
Was that hope false which led us to this place,
Or shall we now behold our sovereign's face?"

The Herald Tells the Birds to Turn Back

The herald said: "This king for whom you grieve
Governs in glory you cannot conceive—
A hundred thousand armies are to Him
An ant that clambers up His threshold's rim,
And what are you? Grief is your fate—go back;
Retrace your steps along the pilgrim's track!"
And when they heard the herald's fearsome words,
An earthly hopelessness assailed the birds.
But they replied: "Our king will not repay
With sorrow all the hazards of the Way;
Grief cannot come to us from majesty;
Grief cannot live beside such dignity. . . .
We told you our desire—if grief must come
Then we are ready and shall not succumb."

The herald said: "The blaze of Majesty
Reduces souls to unreality,
And if your souls are burnt, then all the pain
That you have suffered will have been in vain."
They answered him: "How can a moth flee fire
When fire contains its ultimate desire?
And if we do not join Him, yet we'll burn,
And it is for this for which our spirits yearn—
It is not union for which we hope;
We know that goal remains beyond our scope.". . .
Though grief engulfed the ragged group, love made
The birds impetuous and unafraid;
The herald's self-possession was unmoved,
But their resilience was not reproved—
Now, gently, he unlocked the guarded door;
A hundred veils drew back, and there before
The birds' incredulous, bewildered sight
Shone the unveiled, the inmost Light of Light.
He led them to a noble throne, a place
Of intimacy, dignity and grace,
Then gave them all a written page and said
That when its contents had been duly read
The meaning that their journey had concealed
And of the stage they'd reached, would be revealed. . . .

The Birds Discover the Simorgh

The thirty birds read through the fateful page
And there discovered, stage by detailed stage,
Their lives, their actions, set out one by one—
All that their souls had ever been or done. . . .
Then, as by shame their spirits were refined
Of all the world's weight, they began to find
A new life flow towards them from that bright
Celestial and ever-living Light—
Their souls rose free of all they'd been before;
The past and all its actions were no more.
Their life came from that close, insistent sun
And in its vivid rays they shone as one.
There in the Simorgh's radiant face they saw

Themselves, the Simorgh of the world—with awe
They gazed, and dared at last to comprehend
They were the Simorgh and the journey's end.
They see the Simorgh—at themselves they stare,
And see a second Simorgh standing there;
They look at both and see the two are one,
That this is that, that this, the goal is won.
They ask (but inwardly; they make no sound)
The meaning of these mysteries that confound
Their puzzled ignorance—how is it true
That "we" is not distinguished here from "you"?
And silently their shining Lord replies:
"I am a mirror set before your eyes,
And all who come before my splendor see
Themselves, their own unique reality;
You came as thirty birds and therefore saw
These selfsame thirty birds, not less nor more;
If you had come as forty, fifty—here
An answering forty, fifty, would appear;
Though you have struggled, wandered, traveled far,
It is yourselves you see and what you are. . . .
How much you thought you knew and saw; but you
Now know that all you trusted was untrue.
Though you traversed the Valley's depths and fought
With all the dangers that the journey brought,
The journey was in Me, the deeds were Mine—
You slept secure in Being's inmost shrine.
And since you came as thirty birds, you see
These thirty birds when you discover Me,
The Simorgh, Truth's last flawless jewel, the light
In which you will be lost to mortal sight,
Dispersed to nothingness until once more
You find in Me the selves you were before."
Then, as they listened to the Simorgh's words,
A trembling dissolution filled the birds—
The substance of their being was undone,
And they were lost like shade before the sun;
Neither the pilgrims nor their guide remained.
The Simorgh ceased to speak, and silence reigned.
        Attar, from The Conference of the Birds

One breath from the breath of the lover would be enough to
burn away the world,
To scatter this insignificant universe like grains of sand.
The whole of the cosmos would become a Sea,
And sacred terror rubble this Sea to nothing.
No human being would remain, and no creature:
A smoke would come from heaven: there would be no more
man or angel:
Out of this smoke, flame would suddenly flash out across
heaven.
That second, the sky would split apart and neither space nor
existence remain.
Vast groans would rise up out of the breast of the universe,
groans mingled with desolate moaning,
And fire eat up water, and water eat up fire:
The waves of the Sea of the Void would drown in their flood
the horseman of day and night:
The sun itself fades, vanishes, before this flaming out of the
soul of man.
Do not ask anyone who is not intimate with the secrets
When the intimate of the secret himself cannot answer you.
Mars will lose its swagger, Jupiter burn the book of the
world,
The moon will not hold its empire, its joy will be smirched
with agony.
Mercury will shipwreck in mud, Saturn burn itself to death;
Venus, singer of heaven, play no longer her songs of joy.
The rainbow will flee, and the cup, and the wine,
There will be no more happiness or rapture, no more wound
or cure,
Water will no longer dance with light, wind no longer sweep
the ground,
Gardens no longer abandon themselves to laughter, April's
clouds no longer scatter their dew.
There will be no more grief, no more consolation, no more
"enemy" or "witness,"
No more flute or song, or lute or mode, no more high or low
pitch.

Causes will faint away: the cupbearer will serve himself,
The soul will recite, "O my Lord most high": the heart will
  cry out, "My Lord knows best."
Rise up! The painter of Eternity has set to work one more
  time
To trace miraculous figures on the crazy curtain of the
  world.
God has lit a fire to burn the heart of the universe.
The Sun of God has the East for a heart: the splendor of that
  East
Irradiates at all moments the son of Adam, Jesus, son of
  Mary.
>   *Rumi*

ADMIT IT AND CHANGE EVERYTHING

Define and narrow me, you starve yourself of yourself.
Nail me down in a box of cold words, that box is your
  coffin.
I do not know who I am.
I am in astounded lucid confusion.
I am not a Christian, I am not a Jew, I am not a Zoroastrian,
And I am not even a Muslim.
I do not belong to the land, or to any known or unknown
  sea.
Nature cannot own or claim me, nor can heaven,
Nor can India, China, Bulgaria,
My birthplace is placelessness,
My sign to have and give no sign.
You say you see my mouth, ears, eyes, nose—they are not
  mine.
I am the life of life.
I am that cat, this stone, no one.
I have thrown duality away like an old dishrag,
I see and know all times and worlds,
As one, one, always one.
So what do I have to do to get you to admit who is
  speaking?

Admit it and change everything!
This is your own voice echoing off the walls of God.
      Rumi

SUDDENLY A MOON APPEARED

Suddenly, in the sky at dawn, a moon appeared,
Descended from the sky,
Turned its burning gaze on me,
Like a hawk during the hunt seizing a bird,
Grabbed me and flew with me high into heaven.
When I looked at myself, I could not see myself
For in this moon, my body, by grace, had become soul.
And when I traveled in this soul, I saw nothing but moon,
Until the mystery of eternal theophany lay open to me.
All the nine heavenly spheres were drowned in this moon.
The skiff of my being drowned, dissolved, entirely, in
      that Sea.
Then, that Sea broke up into waves, Intelligence danced
      back,
And launched its song,
And the Sea covered over with foam,
And from each bubble of foam something sprang, clothed in
      form.
Something sprang from each light-bubble, clothed in a body.
Then each bubble of body-foam received a sign from the Sea,
Melted immediately and followed the flow of its waves.
Without the saving, redeeming help of my Lord,
Shams-ul-Haqq of Tabriz,
No one can contemplate the moon, no one can become
      the Sea.
      Rumi

THOUSANDS OF ROSE GARDENS

The intellect says: "The six directions are limits: there is no
      way out."
Love says: "There is a way: I have traveled it thousands of
      times."

The intellect saw a market and started to haggle:
Love saw thousands of markets beyond that market.
Lovers who drink the dregs of the wine reel from bliss to
    bliss:
The dark-hearted men of reason
Burn inwardly with denial.
The intellect says "Do not go forward, annihilation contains
    only thorns."
Love laughs back: "The thorns are in you."
Enough words! Silence!
Pull the thorn of existence out of the heart! Fast!
For when you do you will see thousands of rose gardens in
    yourself.
      Rumi

HURRY TO THE SOURCE OF LIFE

How could the soul not take flight
When from the glorious Presence
A soft call flows sweet as honey, comes right up to her
And whispers, "Rise up now, come away."
How could the fish not jump
Immediately from dry land into water
When the sound of water from the ocean
Of fresh waves springs to his ear?
How could the hawk not fly away
Forgetful of all hunting to the wrist of the king
As soon as he hears the drum
The king's baton hits again and again,
Drumming out the signal of return?
How could the Sufi not start to dance,
Turning on himself, like the atom, in the sun of eternity,
So he can leap free of this dying world?
Fly away, fly away bird to your native home,
You have leapt free of the cage
Your wings are flung back in the wind of God.
Leave behind the stagnant and marshy waters,
Hurry, hurry, hurry O bird, to the Source of Life!
      Rumi

In that moment you are drunk on yourself,
The friend seems a thorn,
In that moment you leap free of yourself, what use is the
    friend?
In that moment you are drunk on yourself,
You are the prey of a mosquito,
And the moment you leap free of yourself, you go elephant
    hunting.
In that moment you are drunk on yourself,
You lock yourself away in cloud after cloud of grief,
And in that moment you leap free of yourself,
The moon catches you and hugs you in its arms.
That moment you are drunk on yourself, the friend aban-
    dons you.
That moment you leap free of yourself, the wine of the
    friend,
In all its brilliance and dazzle, is held out to you.
That moment you are drunk on yourself,
You are withered, withered like autumn leaves.
That moment you leap free of yourself,
Winter to you appears in the dazzling robes of spring.
All disquiet springs from the search for quiet.
Look for disquiet and you will come suddenly on a field of
    quiet.
All illnesses spring from the scavenging for delicacies.
Renounce delicacies and poison itself will seem delicious
    to you.
All disappointments spring from your hunting for satisfac-
    tions.
If only you could stop, all imaginable joys
Would be rolled like pearls to your feet.
Be passionate for the friend's tyranny, not his tenderness,
So the arrogant beauty in you can become a lover that
    weeps.
When the king of the feast, Shams-ud-Din, arrives from
    Tabriz,
God knows you'll be ashamed then of the moon and stars.
    Rumi

The whole world could be choked with thorns:
A lover's heart will stay a rose garden.
The wheel of heaven could wind to a halt:
The world of lovers will go on turning.
Even if every being grew sad, a lover's soul
Will still stay fresh, vibrant, light.
Are all the candles out? Hand them to a lover—
A lover shoots out a hundred thousand fires.
A lover may be solitary, but he is never alone:
For companion he has always the hidden Beloved.
The drunkenness of lovers comes from the soul
And Love's companion stays hidden in secret.
Love cannot be deceived by a hundred promises:
It knows how innumerable the ploys of seducers are.
Wherever you find a lover on a bed of pain—
You find the Beloved right by his bedside.
Mount the stallion of love and do not fear the path—
Love's stallion knows the way exactly.
With one leap, Love's horse will carry you home
However black with obstacles the way may be.
The soul of a real lover spurns all animal fodder,
Only in the wine of bliss can his soul find peace.
Through the Grace of Shams-ud-Din of Tabriz, you will
    possess
A heart at once drunk and supremely lucid.
    Rumi

BORROW THE BELOVED'S EYES

Borrow the Beloved's eyes.
Look through them and you'll see the Beloved's face
everywhere. No tiredness, no jaded boredom.
"I shall be your eye and your hand and your loving."
Let that happen, and things
you have hated will become helpers.

A certain preacher always prays long and with enthusiasm
for thieves and muggers that attack people

on the street. "Let your mercy, O Lord,
cover their insolence."
He doesn't pray for the good,
but only for the blatantly cruel.
Why is this? his congregation asks.

"Because they have done me such generous favors.
Every time I turn back toward the things they want.
I run into them. They beat me and leave me nearly dead
in the road, and I understand, again, that what they want
is not what I want. They keep me on the spiritual path.
That's why I honor them and pray for them."

Those that make you return, for whatever reason,
to God's solitude, be grateful to them.
Worry about the others, who give you
delicious comforts that keep you from prayer.
Friends are enemies sometimes,
and enemies Friends.

There is an animal called an *ushghur*, a porcupine.
If you hit it with a stick, it extends its quills
and gets bigger. The soul is a porcupine,
made strong by stick-beating.
So a prophet's soul is especially afflicted,
because it has to become so powerful.

A hide is soaked in tanning liquor and becomes leather.
If the tanner did not rub in the acid,
the hide would get foul-smelling and rotten.

The soul is a newly skinned hide, bloody and gross.
Work on it with manual discipline,
and the bitter tanning acid of grief,
and you'll become lovely, and *very* strong.

If you can't do this work yourself, don't worry.
You don't even have to make a decision,
one way or another. The Friend, who knows
a lot more than you do, will bring difficulties,
and grief, and sickness, as medicine, as happiness,
as the essence of the moment when you're beaten,

when you hear *Checkmate*, and can finally say,
with Hallaj's voice,
> *I trust you to kill me.*
> Rumi

Seizing my life in your hands, you thrashed it clean
On the savage rocks of Eternal Mind.
How its colors bled, until they grew white!
You smile and sit back; I dry in your sun.

If in hell I could hold one curl of your hair
I'd think the saints of heaven in torment
Called, without you, to the fields of Paradise
Their widest splendors would seem narrow.

Beauty harsher than a thousand suns
Broke into my house, asked "How is your heart?"
His robe of glory trailed the floor; I said
"Pick up your robe; the house is floored with blood"

To meet my thousand thousand faces
I roam my world; the dirtiest grass
Wears the sunlight of my skin:
I stand in this stream, myself, and laugh.

You hide me in your cloak of Nothingness
Reflect my ghost in your glass of Being
I am nothing, yet appear: transparent dream
Where your Eternity briefly trembles

No Heaven or earth, just this mysterious place
We walk in dazedly, where being here
Or there, in time or not, are only
Two motions of the same ecstatic breathing

When Love is in me, I am One with Love
The lightning when I say your name
I roam a dazzled drunkard in our dimension
Where each event is secret laughter

The image in the mirror seems different
But sublime days arrive when you know
Viewer, image, and mirror are one: the same
Silent calm eternal shimmering

One Moon blossoming in a thousand bowls
One Water laughing in a thousand thousand fields
One Sun with a million electric shadows
One Silence with these love-cries for children

Great tree of bliss! Your swaying braziers
Musk each second with Eternity!
I wade incessantly your sea of star-flowers
Your trunk soars blazing from my heart

The law of Wonder rules my life at last
I burn each second of my life to love
Each second of my life burns out in love
In each leaping second love lives afresh
             Rumi, from the Rubaiyat

THE SONG OF VICTORY

When on the day of my death you carry my bier,
Do not imagine my heart has remained in this world.
Do not weep over me, do not say, "How sad, how sad!"
That would be tumbling into the Devil's trap, and that
    would be sad.
When you see my corpse laid out, don't cry out, "He has
    gone,"
For union and meeting will be mine then forever.
As you lower me into my tomb, do not say, "Farewell,"
For the tomb veils from us the union of paradise.
My decline you have seen, now discover my soaring ascent.
Can setting cause any harm to the sun or moon?
To you, my death seems a setting, but really it is dawn.

Does the tomb seem a prison to you? It is the liberation of
    the soul.

Has any seed been sown in the earth that has not one day
    flowered?
Why doubt? Man also is a buried seed.
What bucket would go down empty without being filled?
The spirit is like Joseph, would he complain of the well?
Keep your mouth closed over here, to open it over there
So that beyond space may thrill your song of victory.
> *Rumi*

WHAT A MIRACLE

Glorious is the moment we sit in the palace, you and I
Two forms, two faces, but a single soul, you and I
The flowers will blaze and bird cries shower us with immor-
    tality
The moment we enter the garden, you and I
All the stars of heaven will run out to gaze at us
As we burn as the full moon itself, you and I
The fire-winged birds of heaven will rage with envy
In that place we laugh ecstatically, you and I
What a miracle, you and I, entwined in the same nest
What a miracle, you and I, one love, one lover, one Fire
In this world and the next, in an ecstasy without end.
> *Rumi*

EVERY PARTICLE OF THE WORLD IS A MIRROR

Every particle of the world is a mirror,
In each atom lies the blazing light
    of a thousand suns.
Cleave the heart of a rain-drop,
    a hundred pure oceans will flow forth.
Look closely at a grain of sand,
    the seed of a thousand beings can be seen.
The foot of an ant is larger than an elephant;
In essence, a drop of water
    is no different than the Nile.
In the heart of a barley-corn
    lies the fruit of a hundred harvests;

Within the pulp of a millet seed
   an entire universe can be found.
In the wing of a fly, an ocean of wonder;
   In the pupil of the eye, an endless heaven.
Though the inner chamber of the heart is small,
   the Lord of both worlds
     gladly makes His home there.
      Mahmud Shabestari

COMMENTARY ON SHABESTARI

Shabestari:

Listen with faith to the call: "In all truth, I am God."
He who knows Reality, to whom Unicity is revealed
Sees at first gaze the Light of Being;
He perceives by illumination that pure light;
He sees God first in everything he sees.
Abstraction is the condition of authentic thought
For then the lightning of divine succor illumines us.

On the line "Listen with faith . . ." Lahiji comments:
A *hadith* (sacred saying) of the Prophet declares: "I was a
hidden treasure and I wanted to be known; that is why I created the world." God, in his essence, was in eternity, with His
names and attributes. Nothing then existed—nor does it now—
except Him. Without His perfect manifestation authentic
knowledge is impossible. In short, the essence of Supreme Reality, which is absolute Existence (was hidden), although it is a
pure light. It was necessary that it appears visibly to be a perfect theophany. What is this theophany? The manifestation of
Supreme Reality under the form of archetypes. So what this *hadith* means is that, in reality, both the manifestation *and* the ob-
scuring of the Light are relative.

Through Love has appeared everything that exists
Through Love everything which does not exist appears to.

On the line "He who knows Reality . . ." Lahiji comments:
Shabestari means here that man is the eye of the world, and
that the world is the reflection of God, and that God Himself is
the light of this eye. Man is the eye which looks in the mirror,

and just as the mirror reflects the face of the person who is looking into it, the reflection possesses itself an eye, and in the same time that the eye looks in the mirror, the reflection of this eye looks at it also. God, which is the eye of man, looks at Himself through man.

This point is very subtle: from one side God is the eye of man; from another, man is the eye of the world, because the world and man are only one, man being its eye. This man is called the perfect man. Since man is a resume of everything that exists, he is a world in himself, and the relation that exists between God and man exists between man and the world.

Lahiji

INSPIRATIONS ON THE PATH OF BLAME

Adam said, "I know you not!"

I told him that I had been with him in paradise, but he did not believe me. I told him what had happened to him in the garden when he ate the forbidden fruit—how he had descended from the best of the best to the worst of the worst—and that I had descended with him. I told him how many times he had brought me to earth, and how he took me to himself, and I became human. . . .

Then I told him the story of the pain of Job, who had twelve sons, all exalted and beneficent—who remembered his Lord and worshiped incessantly. One time his enemy and mine, the accursed Devil, came to him in the shape of his shepherd and reported that all of his herds, ten thousand in number, had died of cold; yet Job did not cease praying. The Devil returned as the keeper of his camels and told Job that all had drowned. Job took no notice. Back came the Devil as the foreman of Job's land, announcing that his harvest was ruined. He found no response. In the shape of a maid he came, crying that Job's places were destroyed by an earthquake, his children and people dead. Still the heart of Job did not tighten; he did not forget. As Job prostrated in thankfulness, Satan entered him through his nose and opened gaping holes in his body; yet he could not touch that heart filled with the Lord nor that tongue filled with His names. Job just kept saying, "Praised be the Lord."

I told Adam the story of John the Baptist, the son of Zachariah, who was martyred inside the tree. . . .

I told Adam of Jesus and Moses, Allah's peace and blessings upon them all. And Adam saw it all in himself, the evil in his flesh and the salvation in his soul.

Then I said, "O Adam, let us go within ourselves and watch how the accursed Nimrod is about to throw Abraham into the fire!"

We saw the Devil leading Nimrod, a crowd piling wood onto a pyre. The Devil saw us and commanded Nimrod, "Throw those two in, too!" Nimrod ordered us to be taken, and they brought us with the Prophet Abraham next to the catapult, to cast us into the fire.

Then the Devil came to Abraham. "You claim that there is a god other than Nimrod," he observed. "Deny your claim, and I will have you saved."

I came forward. "O evil one," I exclaimed, "It is not a claim; it is the truth. And you can save no one; you can only lead people astray!"

Satan called to Nimrod, "Destroy them all!"

I threw my cloak on the ground, lifted my staff, and attacked the Devil.

The Devil saw he would have the worst of it. Screaming "Save yourself!" to Nimrod, he turned tail and ran.

I reached out with my two hands and seized the Devil in one and Nimrod in the other. Seeing that I had captured their leaders, all the soldiers fled. I took the two of them and hung them up by their feet from a tree. Adam and the hundred and twenty-four thousand prophets within him cried, "Praise be!"

Now Nimrod, his head hanging down, begged Adam to save him from me. Adam, and all those within him who are close to Allah, told me that Nimrod was not to be blamed. So I took my staff and went to Satan.

"Promise that you will never be the evil-commanding self to me!" I demanded.

"All things existing be my witness: I will never be your evil-commanding self!"

Nimrod assured me that he was ready to be my slave and to do whatever I said.

Then I felt at peace. . . .

And I saw that there was no one but I, no other guest in this temporal inn, and I said, "I am who I know I am."

And I said:

O Lord, is the beloved within the lover?
And the lover in the beloved?
I find not the question why and wherefore.
Am I one within the many?
No, I am the one with the many in me.
I am the owner and the owned,
And the doer and the done.

Now I felt satisfied, for I had all I wished and I knew I could not wish for any more.

Kaygusuz Abdul

8

⌇

Christianity
The Way of Love in Action

One of the most significant results of the revolution of the sacred feminine is that it is leading to a radical reassessment of the Christian tradition. The patriarchal accretions of two thousand years of authoritarian misinterpretation of the Christian message are being discarded to unveil the revelation Christ came to bring again in all its starkness and urgency; Mary is being increasingly turned to not merely as the Mother of God but as the most poignant of all humanity's images of the divine Mother; the witness of the Christian mystics is being increasingly celebrated for its humble accuracy, range, and devotion to the transformation of reality through service. Many Western seekers, like myself, have been on long, complex journeys into the depths and disciplines of Eastern mysticism to find at the end of them a renewed wonder at the Christian inheritance.

One of my hopes for this anthology is that it will deepen this wonder by helping people to see the truths of the other mystical traditions reflected in the depths of the Christian message. The Christian revelation at its richest contains and reflects the Kogi and Hopi knowledge of the interconnection of all life, the Taoist sense of organic balance and the mysterious conjunction of opposites, the Hindu awareness of the grandeur of the soul, the Buddhist devotion to compassion and clear ethical living, the Jewish awe at the unutterable holiness of God and the sacredness of ordinary life, the Greek adoration of divine beauty, and the Islamic passion for God as the Beloved. For me, training in Hindu, Buddhist, and Sufi paths helped me to see just how profound the Christian mystics are and how much a seeker on any path has to learn from them.

Most of all, my own journey has revealed to me how much everyone, whatever their path or religion, has still to learn from the spiritual example of Christ himself. When Mary is known—and increasingly this knowledge is spreading—as the full divine Mother, with all the powers of the Mother, then a largely secret and essential part of Christ's nature is uncovered—that he is as much a son of the Mother as of the Father, and that his message is saturated with the deepest wisdom of the sacred feminine as well as with the truth of the Father, and that in his own life and teaching Christ continues to offer the whole of humankind the most challenging possible example of what it is to live as a divinized sacred androgyne, a fully empowered child of the Father-Mother. And when this new vision of Mary and this new vision of Christ are united (and they are in fact inseparable, because only seeing Mary clearly can help us see Christ in his truth), then the *full* revolutionary nature of their message becomes clear.

This message is very clear when you see it naked, stripped of all the patriarchal body and sex hatred and wholly un-Christlike intolerance and love of authority that have clustered around and deformed it for almost two millennia. It is very clear and very socially and politically radical. It is nothing less than that *all* the terms of the world and its life *must* be transformed to mirror the being and nature of God's overwhelming love for humankind. Christ fuses in his own being the highest "masculine" understanding of the transcendent with the highest "feminine" awareness of the beauty, nobility, and pathos of *this* life, and from this fusion—and from the example of his Mother, who as the Magnificat reminds us was a passionate lover of justice—a vision of the necessity of transformation of *this* world was born.

Perhaps the deepest reason why this vision has been so comprehensively betrayed, especially by those who claim to represent it, is that it is unsparing in its demand. Christ offers his whole being and life as a sacrifice of the most urgent and focused service to all beings and implicitly demands of anyone who loves him the same passion of humble attention and self-donation. Everything is asked and everything must be given if justice is to be done; the facts of social, political, and economic oppression and of the deformity of all kinds of power, including religious power, have to be seen without any consolation; the rigor of a real transformation into love has to be endured; suffering in all its subtle and horribly obvious aspects has to be accepted, embraced, and transformed.

Coming to know Mary as the full divine Mother only deepens the urgency of this demand. Mary, unlike Durga or Kali or Tara, is human, is the human face of the Mother. Far from being the passive figure of patriarchal legend, she was—as any real gaze at the Christian story reveals—a person of extraordinary strength, endurance, and mystical depth, with a deep love of the marginal, the poor, the downtrodden. Coming to know Mary's love is inescapably coming to know Mary's passion for justice, for the transformation of all conditions here on earth into their divine truth.

As we all face the threat of extinction, the demand of Mary, Christ, and of the greatest of their mystical children for us to enact love in every arena of reality and to devote ourselves unstintingly to service of other beings becomes more and more stark, moving, and inescapable.

JESUS' SERMON ON THE MOUNT

And seeing the multitudes, he went up into a mountain: and when he was set, his disciples came unto him:

And he opened his mouth, and taught them, saying,

"Blessed are the poor in spirit: for theirs is the kingdom of heaven.

"Blessed are they that mourn: for they shall be comforted.

"Blessed are the meek: for they shall inherit the earth.

"Blessed are they which do hunger and thirst after righteousness: for they shall be filled.

"Blessed are the merciful: for they shall obtain mercy.

"Blessed are the pure in heart: for they shall see God.

"Blessed are the peacemakers: for they shall be called the children of God.

"Blessed are they which are persecuted for righteousness' sake: for theirs is the kingdom of heaven.

"Blessed are ye, when men shall revile you, and persecute you, and shall say all manner of evil against you falsely, for my sake.

"Rejoice, and be exceeding glad: for great is your reward in heaven: for so persecuted they the prophets which were before you.

"Ye are the salt of the earth: but if the salt have lost his savour, wherewith shall it be salted? it is thenceforth good for nothing, but to be cast out, and to be trodden under foot of men. Ye are the light of the world. A city that is set on an hill cannot be hid.

"Neither do men light a candle, and put it under a bushel, but on a candlestick; and it giveth light unto all that are in the house.

"Let your light so shine before men, that they may see your good works, and glorify your Father which is in heaven."

Matthew 5:1–16

BE YE THEREFORE PERFECT

"Ye have heard that it hath been said, An eye for an eye, and a tooth for a tooth:

"But I say unto you, That ye resist not evil: but whosoever shall smite thee on thy right cheek, turn to him the other also.

"And if any man will sue thee at the law, and take away thy coat, let him have thy cloak also.

"And whosoever shall compel thee to go a mile, go with him twain.

"Give to him that asketh thee, and from him that would borrow of thee turn not thou away.

"Ye have heard that it hath been said, Thou shalt love thy neighbor, and hate thine enemy.

"But I say unto you, Love your enemies, bless them that curse you, do good to them that hate you, and pray for them which despitefully use you, and persecute you;

"That ye may be the children of your Father which is in heaven: for he maketh his sun to rise on the evil and on the good, and sendeth rain on the just and on the unjust.

"For if ye love them which love you, what reward have ye? do not even the publicans the same?

"And if ye salute your brethren only, what do ye more than others? do not even the publicans so?

"Be ye therefore perfect, even as your Father which is in heaven is perfect."

Matthew 5:38–48

"Lay not up for yourselves treasures upon earth, where moth and rust doth corrupt, and where thieves break through and steal:

"But lay up for yourselves treasures in heaven, where neither moth nor rust doth corrupt, and where thieves do not break through nor steal:

"For where your treasure is, there will your heart be also.

"The light of the body is the eye: if therefore thine eye be single, thy whole body shall be full of light. . . .

"No man can serve two masters: for either he will hate the one, and love the other; or else he will hold to the one and despise the other. Ye cannot serve God and Mammon.

"Therefore I say unto you, Take no thought for your life, what ye shall eat, or what ye shall drink; not yet for your body, what ye shall put on. Is not the life more than meat, and the body than raiment?

"Behold the fowls of the air: for they sow not, neither do they reap, nor gather into barns; yet your heavenly Father feedeth them. Are ye not much better than they?

"Which of you by taking thought can add one cubit unto his stature?

"And why take ye thought for raiment? Consider the lilies of the field, how they grow; they toil not, neither do they spin:

"And yet I say unto you, That even Solomon in all his glory was not arrayed like one of these.

"Wherefore, if God so clothe the grass of the field, which today is, and to-morrow is cast into the oven, shall he not much more clothe you, O ye of little faith?

"Therefore take no thought, saying, What shall we eat? or, What shall we drink? or, Wherewithal shall we be clothed?

"(For after all these things do the Gentiles seek:) for your heavenly Father knoweth that ye have need of all these things.

"But seek ye first the kingdom of God, and his righteousness; and all these things shall be added unto you."

Matthew 6:19–22, 24–33

"Ask, and it shall be given you; seek, and ye shall find; knock, and it shall be opened unto you:

"For every one that asketh receiveth; and he that seeketh findeth; and to him that knocketh it shall be opened.

"Or what man is there of you, whom if his son ask bread, will he give him a stone?

"Or if he ask a fish, will he give him a serpent?

"If ye then, being evil, know how to give good gifts unto your children, how much more shall your Father which is in heaven give good things to them that ask him?

"Therefore all things whatsoever ye would that men should do to you, do ye even so to them: for this is the law and the prophets."

Matthew 7:7–12

I WAS THIRSTY AND YOU GAVE ME DRINK

"When the Son of man shall come in his glory, and all the holy angels with him, then shall he sit upon the throne of his glory:

"And before him shall be gathered all nations: and he shall separate them one from another, as a shepherd divideth his sheep from the goats:

"And he shall set the sheep on his right hand, but the goats on the left.

"Then shall the King say unto them on his right hand, 'Come, ye blessed of my Father, inherit the kingdom prepared for you from the foundation of the world:

"'For I was an hungered, and ye gave me meat: I was thirsty, and ye gave me drink: I was a stranger, and ye took me in.

"'Naked, and ye clothed me: I was sick, and ye visited me: I was in prison, and ye came unto me.'

"Then shall the righteous answer him, saying, 'Lord, when saw we thee an hungered, and fed thee? or thirsty, and gave thee drink?

"'When saw we thee a stranger, and took thee in? or naked, and clothed thee?

"'Or when saw we thee sick, or in prison, and came unto thee?

"And the King shall answer and say unto them, 'Verily I say unto you, Inasmuch as ye have done it unto one of the least of these my brethren, ye have done it unto me.'

"Then shall he say also unto them on the left hand, 'Depart from me, ye cursed, into everlasting fire, prepared for the devil and his angels:

"'For I was an hungered, and ye gave me no meat: I was thirsty, and ye gave me no drink:

"'I was a stranger, and ye took me not in: naked, and ye clothed me not: sick, and in prison, and ye visited me not.'

"Then shall they also answer him, saying, 'Lord, when saw we thee an hungered, or athirst, or a stranger, or naked, or sick, or in prison, and did not minister unto thee?'

"Then shall he answer them, saying, 'Verily I say unto you, Inasmuch as ye did it not to one of the least of these, ye did it not to me.'"

Matthew 25:31–45

TAKE UP YOUR CROSS

And when he had called the people unto him with his disciples also, he said unto them, "Whosoever will come after me, let him deny himself, and take up his cross, and follow me.

"For whosoever will save his life shall lose it; but whosoever shall lose his life for my sake and the gospel's, the same shall save it.

"For what shall it profit a man, if he shall gain the whole world, and lose his own soul?"

Mark 8:34–36

BE AS A LITTLE CHILD

And they brought young children to him, that he should touch them: and his disciples rebuked those that brought them.

But when Jesus saw it, he was much displeased, and said unto them, "Suffer the little children to come unto me, and forbid them not: for of such is the kingdom of God.

"Verily I say unto you, Whosoever shall not receive the kingdom of God as a little child, he shall not enter therein."

Mark 10:13–15

"Except a man be born of water and of the Spirit, he cannot enter into the kingdom of God.

"That which is born of the flesh is flesh; and that which is born of the Spirit is spirit.

"Marvel not that I said unto thee, 'Ye must be born again.'

"The wind bloweth where it listeth, and thou hearest the sound thereof, but canst not tell whence it cometh, and whither it goeth: so is every one that is born of the Spirit."

John 3:5–8

BREAD FROM HEAVEN

"Verily, verily, I say unto you, He that believeth on me hath everlasting life.

"I am that bread of life.

"Your fathers did eat manna in the wilderness, and are dead.

"This is the bread which cometh down from heaven, that a man may eat thereof, and not die.

"I am the living bread which came down from heaven: if any man eat of this bread, he shall live for ever: and the bread that I will give is my flesh, which I will give for the life of the world. . . .

"Verily, verily, I say unto you, Except ye eat the flesh of the Son of man, and drink his blood, ye have no life in you.

"Whoso eateth my flesh, and drinketh my blood, hath eternal life; and I will raise him up at the last day.

"For my flesh is meat indeed, and my blood is drink indeed.

"He that eateth my flesh, and drinketh my blood, dwelleth in me, and I in him.

"As the living Father hath sent me, and I live by the Father: so he that eateth me, even he shall live by me.

"This is that bread which came down from heaven: not as your fathers did eat manna, and are dead: he that eateth of this bread shall live for ever."

John 6:47–51, 53–58

"If ye love me, keep my commandments.

"And I will pray the Father, and he shall give you another Comforter, that he may abide with you for ever;

"Even the Spirit of truth; whom the world cannot receive, because it seeth him not, neither knoweth him: but ye know him; for he dwelleth with you, and shall be in you.

"I will not leave you comfortless: I will come to you.

"Yet a little while, and the world seeth me no more; but ye see me: because I live, ye shall live also.

"At that day ye shall know that I am in my Father, and ye in me, and I in you.

"He that hath my commandments, and keepeth them, he it is that loveth me: and he that loveth me shall be loved of my Father, and I will love him, and will manifest myself to him. . . .

"These things have I spoken unto you being yet present with you.

"But the Comforter, which is the Holy Ghost, whom the Father will send in my name, he shall teach you all things and bring all things to your remembrance, whatsoever I have said unto you.

"Peace I leave with you, my peace I give unto you: not as the world giveth, give I unto you. Let not your heart be troubled, neither let it be afraid."

John 14:15–21, 25–27

THE VINE

"I am the true vine, and my Father is the husbandman.

"Every branch in me that beareth not fruit he taketh away: and every branch that beareth fruit, he purgeth it, that it may bring forth more fruit.

"Now ye are clean through the word which I have spoken unto you.

"Abide in me, and I in you. As the branch cannot bear fruit of itself, except it abide in the vine; no more can ye, except ye abide in me.

"I am the vine, ye are the branches: He that abideth in me, and I in him, the same bringeth forth much fruit: for without me ye can do nothing.

"If a man abide not in me, he is cast forth as a branch, and is withered; and men gather them and cast them into the fire, and they are burned.

"If ye abide in me, and my words abide in you, ye shall ask what ye will, and it shall be done unto you.

"Herein is my Father glorified, that ye bear much fruit; so shall ye be my disciples.

"As the Father hath loved me, so have I loved you: continue ye in my love.

"If ye keep my commandments, ye shall abide in my love; even as I have kept my Father's commandments, and abide in his love.

"These things have I spoken unto you, that my joy might remain in you, and that your joy might be full."

> *John 15:1–11*

I IN THEM AND THOU IN ME

Jesus lifted up his eyes to heaven, and said, "Father, the hour is come; glorify thy Son, that thy Son also may glorify thee:

"As thou hast given him power over all flesh, that he should give eternal life to as many as thou hast given him.

"And this is life eternal, that they might know thee the only true God, and Jesus Christ, whom thou hast sent.

"I have glorified thee on the earth: I have finished the work which thou gavest me to do.

"And now, O Father, glorify thou me with thine own self with the glory which I had with thee before the world was.

"I have manifested thy name unto the men which thou gavest me out of the world: thine they were, and thou gavest them me; and they have kept thy word. . . .

"Neither pray I for these alone, but for them also which shall believe on me through their word;

"That they all may be one; as thou, Father, art in me, and I in thee, that they also may be one in us: that the world may believe that thou hast sent me.

"And the glory which thou gavest me I have given them; that they may be one, even as we are one:

"I in them, and thou in me, that they may be made perfect in one; and that the world may know that thou hast sent me, and hast loved them, as thou hast loved me.

"Father, I will that they also, whom thou hast given me, be with me where I am; that they may behold my glory, which thou hast given me: for thou lovedst me before the foundation of the world.

"O righteous Father, the world hath not known thee: but I have known thee, and these have known that thou hast sent me.

"And I have declared unto them thy name, and will declare it: that the love wherewith thou hast loved me may be in them, and I in them."

John 17:1–6, 20–26

Logion 2

Let him who seeks, not cease seeking until he
finds, and when he finds, he will
be troubled, and when he has been troubled, he will
marvel and he will
reign over the All.

Logion 3

Jesus said, "If your leaders say to you, 'Look, the [Father's] imperial rule is in the sky,' then the birds of the sky will precede you. If they say to you, 'It is in the sea,' then the fish will precede you. Rather, the [Father's] imperial rule is inside you and outside you. When you know yourselves, then you will be known, and you will understand that you are children of the living Father. But if you do not know yourselves, then you live in poverty, and you are the poverty."

Logion 22

Jesus saw some babies nursing. He said to his disciples, "These nursing babies are like those who enter the [Father's] domain." They said to him, "Then shall we enter the [Father's] domain as babies?"

Jesus said to them, "When you make the two into one, and when you make the inner like the outer and the outer like the inner, and the upper like the lower, and when you make male and female into a single one, so that the male will not be male nor the female be female, . . . then you will enter [the Father's domain]."

Logion 34

His disciples said, "When will you appear to us, and when will we see you?"

Jesus said, "When you strip without being ashamed, and you take your clothes and put them under your feet like little children and trample them, then [you] will see the son of the living one and you will not be afraid."

Logion 77

I am the Light that is above them all.
I am the All; the All came forth from Me
and the All attained to Me.
Cleave a piece of wood, I am there;
lift up the stone and you will find Me there.

Logion 108

Jesus said, "Whoever drinks from my mouth will become like me; I myself shall become that person, and the hidden things will be revealed to him."

Logion 109

Jesus said, "The [Father's] imperial rule is like a person who had a treasure hidden in his field but did not know it. And [when] he died he left it to his [son]. The son [did] not know [about it either]. He took over the field and sold it. The buyer went plowing, [discovered] the treasure, and began to lend money at interest to whomever he wished."

Logion 113

His disciples said to him, "When will the [Father's] imperial rule come?"

"It will not come by watching for it. It will not be said,
'Look, here!' or 'Look, there!' Rather, the Father's imperial rule
is spread out upon the earth, and people don't see it. "

From the Gospel of Thomas

WE ARE THE CHILDREN OF GOD

The Spirit itself beareth witness with our spirit, that we are the
children of God:

And if children, then heirs; heirs of God, and joint-heirs with
Christ, if so be that we suffer with him, that we may also be
glorified together.

For I reckon that the sufferings of this present time are not
worthy to be compared with the glory which shall be revealed
in us. For the earnest expectation of the creature waiteth for the
manifestation of the sons of God.

For the creature was made subject to vanity, not willingly,
but by reason of him who hath subjected the same in hope,

Because the creature itself also shall be delivered from the
bondage of corruption into the glorious liberty of the children
of God.

For we know that the whole creation groaneth and travaileth
in pain together until now.

And not only they, but ourselves also, which have the first
fruits of the Spirit, even we ourselves groan within ourselves,
waiting for the adoption, to wit, the redemption of our body.

Paul, Romans 8:16–23

BE YE TRANSFORMED

I beseech you therefore, brethren, by the mercies of God, that
ye present your bodies a living sacrifice, holy, acceptable unto
God, which is your reasonable service.

And be not conformed to this world: but be ye transformed
by the renewing of your mind, that ye may prove what is that
good, and acceptable, and perfect, will of God.

For I say, through the grace given unto me, to every man
that is among you, not to think of himself more highly than he

ought to think; but to think soberly, according as God hath dealt to every man the measure of faith.

For as we have many members in one body, and all members have not the same office:

So we, being many, are one body in Christ, and every one members one of another.

Having then gifts differing according to the grace that is given to us, whether prophecy, let us prophesy according to the proportion of faith;

Or ministry, let us wait on our ministering: or he that teacheth, on teaching;

Or he that exhorteth, on exhortation: he that giveth, let him do it with simplicity; he that ruleth, with diligence; he that sheweth mercy, with cheerfulness.

Let love be without dissimulation. Abhor that which is evil; cleave to that which is good.

Paul, Romans 12:1–9

THE FOOLISHNESS OF GOD IS WISER THAN MEN

For the preaching of the cross is to them that perish foolishness; but unto us which are saved it is the power of God.

For it is written, I will destroy the wisdom of the wise, and will bring to nothing the understanding of the prudent.

Where is the wise? where is the scribe? where is the disputer of this world? hath not God made foolish the wisdom of this world?

For after that in the wisdom of God the world by wisdom knew not God, it pleased God by the foolishness of preaching to save them that believe.

For the Jews require a sign, and the Greeks seek after wisdom:

But we preach Christ crucified, unto the Jews a stumbling block, and unto the Greeks foolishness;

But unto them which are called, both Jews and Greeks, Christ the power of God, and the wisdom of God.

Because the foolishness of God is wiser than men; and the weakness of God is stronger than men.

For ye see your calling, brethren, how that not many wise men after the flesh, not many mighty, not many noble, are called:

But God hath chosen the foolish things of the world, to confound the wise; and God hath chosen the weak things of the world, to confound the things which are mighty;

And base things of the world, and things which are despised, hath God chosen, yea, and things which are not, to bring to nought things that are: That no flesh should glory in his presence. . . .

Let no man deceive himself. If any man among you seemeth to be wise in this world, let him become a fool, that he may be wise.

For the wisdom of this world is foolishness with God. For it is written, "He taketh the wise in their own craftiness."

And again, "The Lord knoweth the thoughts of the wise, that they are vain."

Therefore let no many glory in men. For all things are yours;

Whether Paul, or Apollos, or Cephas, or the world, or life, or death, or things present, or things to come; all are yours;

And ye are Christ's; and Christ is God's.

Paul, 1 Corinthians 1:18–29; 3:18–23

I COUNT NOT MYSELF TO HAVE APPREHENDED

But what things were gain to me, those I counted loss for Christ. Yea doubtless, and I count all things but loss for the excellency of the knowledge of Christ Jesus my Lord: for whom I have suffered the loss of all things, and do count them but dung, that I may win Christ,

And be found in him, not having mine own righteousness, which is of the law, but that which is through the faith of Christ, the righteousness which is of God by faith:

That I may know him, and the power of his resurrection, and the fellowship of his sufferings, being made conformable unto his death;

If by any means I might attain unto the resurrection of the dead.

Not as though I had already attained, either were already perfect: but I follow after, if that I may apprehend that for which also I am apprehended of Christ Jesus.

Brethren, I count not myself to have apprehended: but this one thing I do, forgetting those things which are behind, and reaching forth unto those things which are before,

I press toward the mark for the prize of the high calling of God in Christ Jesus.

Let us therefore, as many as be perfect, be thus minded: and if in any thing ye be otherwise minded, God shall reveal even this unto you.

Paul, Philippians 3:7–15

THE GLORY OF CHARITY

Though I speak with the tongues of men and of angels, and have not charity, I am become as sounding brass, or a tinkling cymbal.

And though I have the gift of prophecy, and understand all mysteries, and all knowledge; and though I have all faith, so that I could remove mountains, and have not charity, I am nothing.

And though I bestow all my goods to feed the poor, and though I give my body to be burned, and have not charity, it profiteth me nothing.

Charity suffereth long, and is kind; charity envieth not; charity vaunteth not itself, is not puffed up,

Doth not behave itself unseemly, seeketh not her own, is not easily provoked, thinketh no evil;

Rejoiceth not in iniquity, but rejoiceth in the truth;

Beareth all things, believeth all things, hopeth all things, endureth all things.

Charity never faileth: but whether there be prophecies, they shall fail; whether there be tongues, they shall cease; whether there be knowledge, it shall vanish away.

For we know in part, and we prophesy in part.

But when that which is perfect is come, then that which is in part shall be done away.

When I was a child, I spake as a child, I understood as a child, I thought as a child: but when I became a man, I put away childish things.

For now we see through a glass, darkly; but then face to face: now I know in part; but then shall I know even as also I am known.

And now abideth faith, hope, charity, these three; but the greatest of these is charity.

Paul, 1 Corinthians 13:1–13

A brother in Scete happened to commit a fault, and the elders assembled, and sent for Abbot Moses to join them. He, however, did not want to come. The priest sent him a message, saying: "Come, the community of the brethren is waiting for you." So he arose and started off. And taking with him a very old basket full of holes, he filled it with sand, and carried it behind him. The elders came out to meet him, and said: "What is this, Father?" The elder replied: "My sins are running out behind me, and I do not see them, and today I come to judge the sins of another!" They, hearing this, said nothing to the brother but pardoned him.

A brother asked one of the elders, saying: "There are two brothers, of whom one remains praying in his cell, fasting six days at a time and doing a great deal of penance. The other one takes care of the sick. Which one's work is more pleasing to God?" The elder replied: "If that brother who fasts six days at a time were to hang himself up by the nose, he could not equal the one who takes care of the sick."

Abbot Lot came to Abbot Joseph and said: "Father, according as I am able, I keep my little rule, and my little fast, my prayer, meditation and contemplative silence; and according as I am able I strive to cleanse my heart of thoughts; now what more should I do?" The elder rose up in reply and stretched out his hands to heaven, and his fingers became like ten lamps of fire. He said: "Why not be totally changed into fire?"

From The Desert Fathers

THE DOCTRINE OF INFINITE GROWTH

The great Apostle told the Corinthians of the wonderful visions he enjoyed during the time of his mystical initiation in Paradise—it was a time when he even doubted his own nature, whether he was body or spirit—and he testifies: *I do not count myself to have apprehended. But forgetting the things that are behind, I stretch myself forth to those that are before* (Phil. 3:13). And clearly this is meant to include even that *third heaven* which Paul alone saw; for even Moses told us nothing of it in his cosmogony. Yet even after listening in secret to the mysteries of heaven, Paul does not let the graces he has obtained become the limit of his desire, but he continues to go on and on, never ceasing his ascent. Thus he teaches us, I think, that in our constant participation in the blessed nature of the Good, the graces that we receive at every point are indeed great, but the path that lies beyond our immediate grasp is infinite. This will constantly happen to those who thus share in the divine Goodness, and they will always enjoy a greater and greater participation in grace throughout all eternity.

The pure of heart will see God, according to the Lord's infallible word (Matt. 5:8), according to his capacity, receiving as much as his mind can sustain; yet the infinite and incomprehensible nature of the Godhead remains beyond all understanding. For *the magnificence of His glory*, as the Prophet says, has no end, and as we contemplate Him He remains ever the same, at the same distance above us. The great David enjoyed in his heart those glorious elevations as he progressed from strength to strength; and yet he cried to God: Lord, *thou art the most High*, forever and ever. And by this I think he means that in all the infinite eternity of centuries, the man who runs toward Thee constantly becomes greater as he rises higher, ever growing in proportion to his increase in grace. *Thou*, indeed, *art the most High*, abiding forever, and canst never seem smaller to those who approach Thee for Thou art always to the same degree higher and loftier than the faculties of those who are rising.

This, then, is the doctrine that I think the Apostle is teaching about the ineffable nature of the Good, when he says that the eye does not know it even though it may see it. For the eye does not see it completely as it is, but only insofar as it can receive it. So too, even though we may constantly listen to the Word, we do not hear it completely according to its manifestation. And even though the clean of heart use his eyes as much as he can, yet it has not *entered into the heart of man*. Thus though the new grace we may obtain is greater than what we had before, it does not put a limit on our final goal; rather, for those who are rising in perfection, the limit of the good that is attained becomes the beginning of the discovery of higher goods. Thus they never stop rising, moving from one new beginning to the next, and the beginning of ever greater graces is never limited of itself. For the desire of those who thus rise never rests in what they can already understand; but by an ever greater and greater desire, the soul keeps rising constantly to another which lies ahead, and thus it makes its way through ever higher regions towards the Transcendent.

Gregory of Nyssa

UNITY IN DIVERSITY

All that the Father is, we see revealed in the Son; all that is the Son's is the Father's also; for the whole Son dwells in the Father, and he has the whole Father dwelling in himself. . . . The Son who exists always in the Father can never be separated from him, nor can the Spirit ever be divided from the Son who through the Spirit works all things. He who receives the Father also receives at the same time the Son and the Spirit. It is impossible to envisage any kind of severance or disjunction between them: one cannot think of the Son apart from the Father, nor divide the Spirit from the Son. There is between the three a sharing and a differentiation that are beyond words and understanding.

The distinction between the persons does not impair the oneness of nature, nor does the shared unity of essence lead to a confusion between the distinctive characteristics of the persons. Do not be surprised that we should speak of the Godhead as being at the same time both unified and differentiated. Using riddles, as it were, we envisage a strange and paradoxical diversity-in-unity and unity-in-diversity.

Gregory of Nyssa

Trinity!! Higher than any being,
    any divinity, any goodness!

Guide of Christians
in the wisdom of heaven!
Lead us up beyond unknowing and light,
up to the farthest, highest peak
of mystic scripture,
where the mysteries of God's Word
lie simple, absolute and unchangeable
in the brilliant darkness of a hidden silence.
Amid the deepest shadow
they pour overwhelming light
on what is most manifest.
Amid the wholly unsensed and unseen
they completely fill our sightless minds
with treasures beyond all beauty.

Leave the senses and the workings of the intellect, and all that
the sense and the intellect can perceive, and all that is not and
that is; and through unknowing reach out, so far as this is possible, toward oneness with him who is beyond all being and
knowledge. In this way, through an uncompromising, absolute
and pure detachment from yourself and from all things, tran-
scending all things and released from all, you will be led upwards toward that radiance of the divine darkness which is
beyond all being.

Entering the darkness that surpasses understanding, we shall
find ourselves brought, not just to brevity of speech, but to perfect silence and unknowing.

Emptied of all knowledge, man is joined in the highest part
of himself, not with any created thing, nor with himself, nor
with another, but with the One who is altogether unknowable;
and in knowing nothing, he knows in a manner that surpasses
understanding.

Dionysius the Areopagite

ENTERING INTO JOY

Imagine if all the tumult of the body were to quiet down,
along with all our busy thoughts about earth, sea, and air;

if the very world should stop, and the mind cease thinking
about itself, go beyond itself, and be quite still;

if all the fantasies that appear in dreams and imagination
should cease, and there be no speech, no sign:

Imagine if all things that are perishable grew still—
for if we listen they are saying, "We did not make ourselves;
he made us who abides forever"—imagine, then, that they
should say this and fall silent, listening to the very voice
of him who made them and not to that of his creation;

so that we should hear not his word through the tongues
of men, nor the voice of angels, nor the clouds' thunder,
nor any symbol, but the very Self which in these things
we love, and go beyond ourselves to attain a flash of that
eternal wisdom which abides above all things:

And imagine if that moment were to go on and on,
leaving behind all other sights and sounds but this one
vision which ravishes and absorbs and fixes the beholder
in joy; so that the rest of eternal life were like that
moment of illumination which leaves us breathless:

Would this not be what is bidden in scripture, Enter thou
into the joy of thy Lord?
    Saint Augustine

AKATHIST HYMN TO THE VIRGIN

Hail to you through whom joy will shine out!
Hail, redemption of fallen Adam!
Hail, deliverance of the tears of Eve!
Hail, height unattainable by human thought!
Hail, depth invisible even to the eyes of angels! . . .

Hail, lightning that lights up our souls!
Hail, star that causest the sun to appear!
Hail, thou through whom the creation becomes man!
Hail, bridge that conveys us from earth to heaven!
Hail, access of mortals to God!
Hail, defense against invisible enemies!
Hail, key to the gates of paradise!
Hail, radiant blaze of grace!

Hail, thou through whom we are clothed in glory!
Hail, pillar of the fire guiding those in darkness!
Hail, key to the kingdom of Christ!
Hail, impregnable wall of the kingdom!
Hail, thou through whom we obtain our victories!
Hail, healing of my body!
Hail, salvation of my soul!

Romanus the Melodist

I know the Immovable comes down;
I know the Invisible appears to me;
I know that he who is far outside the whole creation
Takes me within himself and hides me in his arms,
And then I find myself outside the whole world.
I, a frail, small mortal in the world,
Behold the Creator of the world, all of him, within myself;
And I know I shall not die, for I am within Life,
I have the whole of Life springing up as a fountain within me.
He is in my heart, he is in heaven:
Both there and here he shows himself to me with equal glory.

Symeon the New Theologian

LED TO THE DESERT

Consider the divine spirit in the human soul.
This spirit is not easily satisfied.
It storms the firmament
and scales the heavens
trying to reach the Spirit that drives the heavens.
Because of this energy
everything in the world grows green,
flourishes,
and bursts into leaf.
But the spirit is never satisfied.
It presses on
deeper and deeper into the vortex
further and further into the whirlpool,
the primary source
in which the spirit has its origin.

This spirit seeks to be
broken through by God.
God leads this spirit
into a desert
into the wilderness and solitude of the divinity
where God is pure unity
and where God gushes up within himself.
Meister Eckhart

SERMON NINETEEN: SURREXIT AUTEM SAULUS DE TERRA
APERTISQUE OCULIS NIHIL VIDEBAT

This text which I have quoted in Latin is written by St. Luke in
Acts about St. Paul. It means: "Paul rose from the ground and
with open eyes saw nothing."

I think this text has a fourfold sense. One is that when he
rose up from the ground with open eyes he saw Nothing, and
the Nothing was God; for when he saw God he calls that Nothing. The second: when he got up he saw nothing but God. The
third: in all things he saw nothing but God. The fourth: when
he saw God, he saw all things as nothing. . . .

"Paul rose from the ground and with open eyes saw nothing.". . .

A master says whoever speaks of God in any likeness, speaks
impurely of Him. But to speak of God with nothing is to speak
of Him correctly. When the soul is unified and there enters into
total self-abnegation, then she finds God as in Nothing. It appeared to a man as in a dream—it was a waking dream—that
he became pregnant with Nothing like a woman with child,
and in that Nothing God was born, He was the fruit of nothing. God was born in the Nothing. . . .

If we are to know God it must be without means, and then
nothing alien can enter in. If we do see God in this light, it must
be quite private and indrawn, without the intrusion of anything
created. Then we have an immediate knowledge of eternal
life. . . .

For God to be perceived by the soul, she must be blind.
Therefore, he says, "He saw the Nothing," from whose light all
lights come, from whose essence all essence comes. And so the
bride says in the Book of Love: "When I had passed on a little

further, I found Him that my soul loves." The little that she passed by was all creatures. Whoever does not put them behind him will not find God. She also means that however subtle, however pure a thing is that I know God by, yet it must go. Even the light that is truly God, if I take it where it touches my soul, that is still not right. I must take it there, where it wells forth. I could not properly see the light that shines on the wall unless I turned my gaze to where it comes from. And even then, if I take it where it wells forth, I must be free of this welling forth: I must take it where it rests in itself. And yet I say even that is wrong. I must take it neither where it touches nor where it wells forth nor where it rests in itself, for these are still all modes. We must take God as mode without mode, and essence without essence, for He has no modes. Therefore St. Bernard says, "He who would know thee, God, must measure thee without measure."

Let us pray to our Lord that we may come to that understanding that is wholly without mode and without measure.

Meister Eckhart

IN YOUR MIDST

I, God, am in your midst.
Whoever knows me can never fall,
   Not in the heights,
   Nor in the depths,
   Nor in the breadths,
   For I am love,
Which the vast expanses of evil
   Can never still.
     Hildegard of Bingen

Lord, make me an instrument of thy peace.
Where there is hatred, let me sow love;
Where there is injury, pardon;
Where there is doubt, faith;
Where there is despair, hope;
Where there is darkness, light;
Where there is sadness, joy.

O divine Master, grant that I may not so much seek
To be consoled as to console,
To be understood as to understand,
To be loved as to love;
For it is in giving that we receive;
It is in pardoning that we are pardoned;
It is in dying to self that we are born to eternal life.
Francis of Assisi

All Glory to You, most high, omnipotent, and good Lord
Praise and honor forever, and every blessing.
To You alone, most high One, should these be given
And no man is worthy of naming You.
Glory to You, my Lord, for all Your creatures
Especially our brother, the sun,
Who is the day, and by whom You give us light:
He is beautiful and radiant with great splendor
And bears witness to You, most high One.
Glory to You, my Lord, for sister moon and the stars
You have made in heaven clear, precious, and beautiful.
Glory to You, my Lord, for brother wind
And for air and cloud and serene sky
And all the different weathers
By which You sustain all creatures.
Glory to You, my Lord, for sister water
Who is very useful and humble
And precious and pure.
Glory to You, my Lord, for brother fire
By whom You illumine night
And he is beautiful and joyful and robust and full of power.
Glory to You, my Lord, for sister our mother earth
Who sustains and governs us
And produces different fruits
And brightly colored flowers and grass.
Glory to You, my Lord,
For those who forgive for love of You

And bear sicknesses and ordeals.
Happy are those who bear them in peace
For they will be crowned by You, most high Lord.
Glory be to You, my Lord,
For our sister bodily death
From whom no living man can escape.
Grief to all those who die
In mortal sin—
Happy those whom death will find
Firm in Your holy will—
The second death will do them no harm.
Praise and bless my Lord
Be grateful to Him,
And serve Him in great humility.

       Francis of Assisi

HOW THE SOUL THROUGH THE SENSES FINDS GOD IN ALL CREATURES

O Love, divine Love, why do You lay siege to me?
In a frenzy of love for me, You find no rest.

From five sides You move against me,
Hearing, sight, taste, touch, and scent.
To come out is to be caught; I cannot hide from You.

If I come out through sight I see Love
Painted in every form and color,
Inviting me to come to You, to dwell in You.

If I leave through the door of hearing,
What I hear points only to You, Lord;
I cannot escape Love through this gate.

If I come out through taste, every flavor proclaims:
"Love, divine Love, hungering Love!
You have caught me on Your hook, for You want to reign
   in me."

If I leave through the door of scent
I sense You in all creation; You have caught me
And wounded me through that fragrance.

If I come out through the sense of touch
I find Your lineaments in every creature;
To try to flee from You is madness.

Love, I flee from You, afraid to give You my heart:
I see that You make me one with You,
I cease to be me and can no longer find myself.

If I see evil in a man or defect or temptation,
You fuse me with him, and make me suffer;
O Love without limits, who is it You love?

It is You, O Crucified Christ,
Who take possession of me,
Drawing me out of the sea to the shore;

There I suffer to see Your wounded heart.
Why did You endure the pain?
So that I might be healed.

Jacopone da Todi

CHRIST THE MOTHER

I saw that he is to us everything which is good and comforting
for our help. He is our clothing, who wraps and enfolds us for
love, embraces us and shelters us, surrounds us for his love,
which is so tender that he may never desert us. . . . And in this
he showed me something small, no bigger than a hazelnut,
lying in the palm of my hand, as it seemed to me, and it was as
round as a ball. I looked at it with the eye of my understanding
and thought: what can this be? I was amazed that it could last,
for I thought that because of its littleness it would suddenly
have fallen into nothing. And I was answered in my understanding: It lasts and always will, because God loves it; and
thus everything has being through the love of God. . . .

Our Mother in nature, our Mother in grace, because he
wanted altogether to become our Mother in all things, made
the foundation of his work most humbly and most mildly in the
maiden's womb. . . . The mother's service is nearest, readiest
and surest: nearest because it is most natural, readiest because

it is most loving, and surest because it is truest. No one ever might or could perform this office fully, except only for him. We know that all our mothers bear us for pain and for death. O, what is that? But our true Mother Jesus, he alone bears us for joy and for endless life, blessed may he be. So he carries us within him in love and travail, until the full time when he wanted to suffer the sharpest thorns and cruel pains that ever were or will be, and at last he died. . . .

The mother can lay her child tenderly to her breast, but our tender Mother Jesus can lead us easily into his blessed breast through his sweet open side, and show us there a part of the godhead and of the joys of heaven, with inner certainty of endless bliss. . . .

This fair, lovely word "mother" is so sweet and so kind in itself that it cannot truly be said of anyone or to anyone except of him and to him who is the true Mother of life and of all things.

Juliana of Norwich

MARY, STAR OF THE SEA

O you, whoever you are, who feel that in the tidal wave of this world you are nearer to being tossed about among the squalls and gales than treading on dry land, if you do not want to founder in the tempest, do not avert your eyes from the brightness of this star. When the wind of temptation blows up within you, when you strike upon the rock of tribulation, gaze up at this star, call out to Mary. Whether you are being tossed about by the waves of pride or ambition or slander or jealousy, gaze up at this star, call out to Mary. When rage or greed or fleshly desires are battering the skiff of your soul, gaze up at Mary. When the immensity of your sins weighs you down and you are bewildered by the loathsomeness of your conscience, when the terrifying thought of judgment appalls you and you begin to founder in the gulf of sadness and despair, think of Mary. In dangers, in hardships, in every doubt, think of Mary, call out to Mary. Keep her in your mouth, keep her in your heart. Follow the example of her life and you will obtain the favor of her prayer. Following her, you will never go astray. Asking her help, you will never despair. Keeping her in your thoughts, you will never wander away. With your hand in hers, you will never stumble. With her protecting you, you will not be afraid. With her leading you, you will never tire. Her kindness will see you through to the end.

Bernard of Clairvaux

God Speaks to the Soul

And God said to the soul:
I desired you before the world began.
I desire you now
As you desire me.
And where the desires of two come together
There love is perfected.

How the Soul Speaks to God

Lord, you are my lover,
My longing,
My flowing stream,
My sun,
And I am your reflection.

How God Answers the Soul

It is my nature that makes me love you often,
For I am love itself.
It is my longing that makes me love you intensely,
For I yearn to be loved from the heart.
It is my eternity that makes me love you long,
For I have no end.

Mechthild of Magdeburg

All things
are too small
to hold me,
I am so vast

In the Infinite
I reach
for the Uncreated

I have
touched it,
it undoes me
wider than wide

Everything else
is too narrow

You know this well,
you who are also there
Hadewijch of Antwerp

BEHOLD MY HUMILITY

The eyes of my soul were opened, and I beheld the plenitude of
God, wherein I did comprehend the whole world, both here
and beyond the sea, and the abyss and ocean and all things. In
all these things I beheld naught save the divine power, in a manner assuredly indescribable; so that through excess of marveling
the soul cried with a loud voice, saying, "This whole world is
full of God!" Wherefore I now comprehended how small a
thing is the whole world, that is to say both here and beyond
the seas, the abyss, the ocean, and all things; and that the
Power of God exceeds and fills all. Then He said unto me: "I
have shown thee something of My Power," and I understood,
that after this I should better understand the rest. He then said,
"Behold now My humility." Then was I given an insight into
the deep humility of God toward man. And comprehending
that unspeakable power and beholding that deep humility, my
soul marveled greatly, and did esteem itself to be nothing at all.
Angela of Foligno

THE SOUL AS A LIVING MIRROR

At the beginning of the world, when God resolved to create the
first human being, he said in the Trinity of Persons: "Let us
make man to our image and to our likeness" (Gen. 1:26). God
is a spirit, so his word is his knowledge and his action is his
will. He is able to do all that he wills, and all his acts are full of

grace and good order. He has created each person's soul as a living mirror, on which he has impressed the image of his nature. In this way he lives imaged forth in us and we in him, for our created life is one, without intermediary, with this image and life which we have eternally in God. That life which we have in God is one in God, without intermediary, for it lives in the Father with the unbegotten Son and is begotten with the Son from the Father, flowing forth from them both with the Holy Spirit. We thus live eternally in God and he in us, for our created being lives in our eternal image, which we have in the Son of God. This eternal image is one with God's wisdom and lives in our created being.

For this reason the eternal birth is always being renewed, and the flowing forth of the Holy Spirit into the emptiness of our soul is always occurring without interruption, for God has known, loved, called, and chosen us from all eternity. If we resolve to know, love, and choose him in return, then we are holy, blessed, and chosen from all eternity. Our heavenly Father will then reveal his divine resplendence in the topmost part of our soul, for we are his kingdom, in which he lives and reigns. Just as the sun in the heavens pervades and enlightens all the world with its rays and makes it fruitful, so too does God's resplendence as it reigns in the topmost part of our mind, for upon all our powers it sheds its bright, brilliant rays, namely, its divine gifts: knowledge, wisdom, clear understanding, and a rational, discerning insight into all the virtues. It is in this way that the kingdom of God in our soul is adorned.

For its part, that infinite love which is God himself reigns in the purity of our spirit like the glow of burning coals. It sends forth brilliant, burning sparks which, in the fire of love, touch and enflame the heart and senses, the will and desires, and all the powers of the soul to a stormy transport of restless, formless love. These are the weapons with which we must do battle against the awesome, immense love of God, which strives to burn up and devour all loving spirits in their very being. Nevertheless God's love arms us with its own gifts, enlightening our reason and commanding, advising, and teaching us to defend ourselves in the struggle and to maintain our own rights in love against it as long as we can. For this purpose it gives us fortitude, knowledge, and wisdom, and it draws all our sensible powers together into an experience of interior fervor. It makes our heart love, desire, and savor, gives our soul the power to fix its gaze in contemplation, bestows upon us the gift of devotion, and makes us ascend on its fiery flames. It also gives knowledge and the taste of eternal wisdom to our understanding, touches our amorous power, and makes our spirit burn and melt away in veneration before its face.

Here our reason and every activity characterized by the making of distinctions must give way, for our powers now become simply one in love, grow silent, and incline toward the Father's face, since this revelation of the Father raises the soul above reason to a state of imageless bareness. There the soul is simple, spotless, and pure, empty of everything. In this pure emptiness the Father reveals his divine resplendence, which neither reason nor the senses, neither rational observation nor distinctions can attain. Rather, all these things must remain below, for this infinite resplendence so blinds the eyes of reason that they have to give way before this incomprehensible light. However, that simple eye which dwells above reason in the ground of our understanding is always open, contemplating with unhindered vision and gazing at the light with the light itself—eye to eye, mirror to mirror, image to image.

With these three—eye, mirror, and image—we are like God and united with him, for this vision in our simple eye is a living mirror which God created to his image and on which he impressed his image. His image is his divine resplendence, with which he fills the mirror of our soul to overflowing, so that no other light or image can enter there. But this resplendence is not an intermediary between God and ourselves, for it is both the very thing which we see and also the light with which we see, though it is distinct from our eye which does the seeing. Even though God's image is in the mirror of our soul and is united with it without intermediary, still the image is not the mirror, for God does not become a creature. The union of the image in the mirror is, however, so great and so noble that the soul is called the image of God.

John Ruusbroec

The Divine Persons who form one sole God, are in the fecundity of their nature ever active: and in the simplicity of their essence they form the Godhead and eternal blessedness. Thus God according to the Persons is Eternal Work: but according to the essence and Its perpetual stillness, He is Eternal Rest. Now love and fruition live between this activity and this rest. . . .

Our activity consists in loving God and our fruition in enduring God and being penetrated by His love. There is a distinction between love and fruition, as there is between God and His Grace. When we unite ourselves to God by love, then we are spirit: but when we are caught up and transformed by His Spirit, then we are led into fruition. And the spirit of God Himself breathes us out from Himself that we may love, and may do good works; and again He draws us into Himself, that we may rest in fruition. And this is Eternal Life; even as our mortal life subsists in the indrawing and outgoing of our breath. . . .

Understand, God comes to us incessantly, both with means and without means; and He demands of us both action and fruition, in such a way that the action never hinders the fruition, nor the fruition the action, but they strengthen one another. And this is why the interior man lives his life according to these two ways; that is to say, in rest and in work. And in each of them he is wholly and undividedly; for he dwells wholly in God in virtue of his restful fruition and wholly in himself in virtue of his active love. And God, in His communications, perpetually calls and urges him to renew both this rest and this work. And because the soul is just, it desires to pay at every instant that which God demands of it; and this is why each time it is irradiated of Him, the soul turns inward in a manner that is both active and fruitive, and thus it is renewed in all virtues and ever more profoundly immersed in fruitive rest. . . .

The soul is active in all loving work, for it sees its rest. It is a pilgrim, for it sees its country. For love's sake it strives for victory, for it sees its crown. Consolation, peace, joy, beauty and riches, all that can give delight, all this is shown to the mind illuminated in God, in spiritual similitudes and without measure. And through this vision and touch of God, love continues active. For such a just man has built up in his soul, in rest and in

work, a veritable life which shall endure forever. . . . Thus this
man is just, and he goes toward God by inward love, in eternal
work, and he goes in God by his fruitive inclination in eternal
rest. And he dwells in God; and yet he goes out toward all creatures, in a spirit of love toward all things, in virtue and in
works of righteousness. And this is the supreme summit of the
inner life.

John Ruusbroec

DARK NIGHT

On a dark secret night,
starving for love and deep in flame,
O happy lucky flight!
unseen I slipped away,
my house at last was calm and safe.

Blackly free from light,
disguised and down a secret way,
O happy lucky flight!
in darkness I escaped,
my house at last was calm and safe.

On that happy night—in
secret; no one saw me through the dark—
and I saw nothing then,
no other light to mark
the way but fire pounding my heart.

That flaming guided me
more firmly than the noonday sun,
and waiting there was he
I knew so well—who shone
where nobody appeared to come.

O night, my guide!
O night more friendly than the dawn!
O tender night that tied
lover and the loved one,
loved one in the lover fused as one!

On my flowering breasts
which I had saved for him alone,
he slept and I caressed
and fondled him with love,
and cedars fanned the air above.

Wind from the castle wall
while my fingers played in his hair:
its hand serenely fell
wounding my neck, and there
my senses vanished in the air.

I lay. Forgot my being,
and on my love I leaned my face.
All ceased. I left my being,
leaving my cares to fade
among the lilies far away.
        John of the Cross

THE FOUNTAIN

How well I know that flowing spring
    in black of night.

The eternal fountain is unseen.
How well I know where she has been
    in black of night.

I do not know her origin.
None. Yet in her all things begin
    in black of night.

I know that nothing is so fair
and earth and firmament drink there
    in black of night.

I know that none can wade inside
to find her bright bottomless tide
    in black of night.

Her shining never has a blur;
I know that all light comes from her
    in black of night.

I know her streams converge and swell
and nourish people, skies and hell
    in black of night.

The stream whose birth is in this source
I know has a gigantic force
    in black of night.

The stream from but these two proceeds
yet neither one, I know, precedes
    in black of night.

The eternal fountain is unseen
in living bread that gives us being
    in black of night.

She calls on all mankind to start
to drink her water, though in dark,
    for black is night.

O living fountain that I crave,
in bread of life I see her flame
    in black of night.
              John of the Cross

THE BRIDE SPEAKS OF HER LOVE

Our flowery bed is safely
hidden among the lion caves,
under a purple tent
erected in deep peace
and capped with a thousand gold shields.

Young girls wander about
the roads seeking a sign from you
in the falling lightning
or in the scented wine
which emanates a holy balm.

Deep in the winevault of
my love I drank, and when I came
out on this open meadow

I knew no thing at all,
I lost the flock I used to drive.

He held me to his chest
and taught me a sweet science.
Instantly I yielded all
I had—keeping nothing—
and promised then to be his bride.

I gave my soul to him
and all the things I owned were his:
I have no flock to tend
nor any other trade
and my one ministry is love.

If I'm no longer seen
following sheep about the hills,
say that I am lost, that
wandering in love I let
myself be lost and then was won.

John of the Cross, from The Spiritual Canticle

I saw an angel close by me, on my left side in bodily form. This I am not accustomed to see unless very rarely. Though I have visions of angels frequently, yet I see them only by an intellectual vision, such as I have spoken of before. It was our Lord's will that in this vision I should see the angel in this wise. He was not large, but small of stature, and most beautiful—his face burning, as if he were one of the highest angels, who seem to be all of fire: they must be those whom we call Cherubim. . . . I saw in his hand a long spear of gold, and at the iron's point there seemed to be a little fire. He appeared to me to be thrusting it at times into my heart, and to pierce my very entrails; when he drew it out, he seemed to draw them out also and to leave me all on fire with a great love of God. The pain was so great that it made me moan; and yet so surpassing was the sweetness of this excessive pain that I could not wish to be rid of it. The soul is satisfied now with nothing less than God. The pain is not bodily, but spiritual; though the body has its share in it, even a large one. It is a caressing of love so sweet which now takes place between the soul and God, that I pray God of His goodness to make him experience it who may think that I am lying.

Teresa of Avila

MARY AND MARTHA MUST COMBINE

Do you suppose St. Paul hid himself in order to enjoy in peace these spiritual consolations, and did nothing else? You know that on the contrary he never took a day's rest so far as we can learn and worked at night in order to earn his bread. . . . Oh my sisters! how forgetful of her own ease, how careless of honors, should she be whose soul God thus chooses for His special dwelling place! For if her mind is fixed on Him, as it ought to be, she must needs forget herself; all her thoughts are bent on how to please Him better, and when and how she may show Him her love. This is the end and aim of prayer, my daughters; this is the object of that spiritual marriage whose children are always good works. Works are the best proof that the favors which we receive have come from God. To give our Lord a perfect hospitality. . . Mary and Martha must combine.

Teresa of Avila

YOU ARE CHRIST'S HANDS

Christ has no body now on earth but yours,
   no hands but yours,
   no feet but yours,
Yours are the eyes through which is to look out
   Christ's compassion to the world
Yours are the feet with which he is to go about
   doing good;
Yours are the hands with which he is to bless men now.

Teresa of Avila

THE HOUSE OF GOD

Your enjoyment of the world is never right, till every morning you awake in Heaven; see yourself in your Father's Palace; and look upon the skies, the earth, and the air as Celestial Joys:

having such a reverend esteem of all, as if you were among the Angels. The bride of a monarch, in her husband's chamber, hath no such causes of delight as you.

You never enjoy the world aright, till the Sea itself floweth in your veins, till you are clothed with the heavens, and crowned with the stars: and perceive yourself to be the sole heir of the whole world, and more than so, because men are in it who are every one sole heirs as well as you. Till you can sing and rejoice and delight in God, as misers do in gold, and Kings in scepters, you never enjoy the world.

Till your spirit filleth the whole world, and the stars are your jewels; till you are as familiar with the ways of God in all Ages as with your walk and table: till you are intimately acquainted with that shady nothing out of which the world was made: till you love men so as to desire their happiness, with a thirst equal to the zeal of your own; till you delight in God for being good to all: you never enjoy the world. Till you more feel it than your private estate, and are more present in the hemisphere, considering the glories and the beauties there, than in your own house: Till you remember how lately you were made, and how wonderful it was when you came into it: and more rejoice in the palace of your glory, than if it had been made but today morning.

Yet further, you never enjoy the world aright, till you so love the beauty of enjoying it, that you are covetous and earnest to persuade others to enjoy it. . . . The world is a mirror of infinite beauty, yet no man sees it. It is a Temple of Majesty, yet no man regards it. It is a region of Light and Peace, did not men disquiet it. It is the Paradise of God. It is more to man since he is fallen than it was before. It is the place of Angels and the Gate of Heaven. When Jacob waked out of his dream, he said "God is here, and I wist it not. How dreadful is this place! This is none other than the House of God and the Gate of Heaven."

Thomas Traherne, from Centuries of Meditation

True Blessing

Nothing is imperfect, the pebble equals the ruby
A frog is as beautiful as any seraphim.

In God All Is God

In God all is God; the simplest little worm
Is as much in God as thousands of Gods.

I Am as Vast as God

I am as vast as God; there is nothing in the world
O Miracle:—that can shut me up in myself.

As Much as God

I am as much as God, there isn't a grain of dust
I do not share—believe me—with Him entirely.

You Must Be Sun

I must be sun and paint with my own rays
The color-free Sea of total Godhead.

God Blossoms in His Branches

If you are born in God, in you God will blossom—
His Godhead will be your sap and flower.

You Must Be the Essence

Love is difficult, because loving is not enough:
We must, like God, ourselves be Love.

Godhead Is Greenness

Godhead is my sap; what greens and blooms from me
Springs from His Holy Spirit, the force of flowering.

Wisdom

Wisdom laughs to be where her children are—
Why? O Miracle! She herself is a child.

Christ Is Everything

O Miracle! Christ is the Truth and the Word
Is Light, life, meal, path, pilgrim, place and door.

Necessary Humility

Keep your eyes on the ground; you flee the lightning of time
How could you stand the lightning of Eternity?

Man Is Nothing, God Is Everything

I am not I nor You; You are myself in me.
That is why I give you, God, all the glory.

God Works Like a Fire

Fire melts and makes One; if you rejoin Origin
Your spirit with God's will be melted in One.
Angelus Silesius

MARY AND THE SECOND COMING OF CHRIST

It is through the Very Holy Virgin that Jesus Christ came into
the world to begin with, and it is also through her that he will
reign in the world. . . .

I say with the saints; the divine Mary is the terrestrial paradise of the New Adam, where he was incarnate by the operation of the Holy Spirit to work incomprehensible miracles, she
is the great, divine world of God where there are ineffable
beauties and treasures. She is the magnificence of the Most
High where He has hidden, as if in His own breast, his only
Son. . . . Oh! How many great and hidden things all-powerful
God has made in this wonderful woman. . . .

Until now, the divine Mary has been unknown, and this is
one of the reasons why Jesus Christ is hardly known as he
should be. If then—as is certain—the knowledge and reign of
Jesus Christ arrive in the world, it will be a necessary conse-

quence of the knowledge and reign of the Very Holy Virgin, who birthed him into this world the first time and will make him burst out everywhere the second.

Jesus Christ is for every person who possesses him the fruit and the work of Mary. . . . When Mary has put down her roots in a soul she engenders there miracles of grace that she alone can work, for she alone is the fecund Virgin who has never had and never will have any equal in purity or fecundity. . . . Mary has produced, with the Holy Spirit, the greatest thing that has ever been—or will ever be—the God-man, and she will produce the greatest things that shall be in these last times. The formation and education of the heroic saints that will come at the end of the world are reserved for her; for only this singular and miraculous Virgin can produce, in union with the Holy Spirit, singular and extraordinary things. . . .

Mary must break out more than ever in these last times in pity, force, and grace. Her power over the demons will flash out everywhere. . . . It is a kind of miracle when a person remains firm in the middle of the fierce torrent of these times, and stays uninfected in the plague-ridden air of our corrupt era. . . . It is the Virgin, in whom the Serpent has never had any part, that works this miracle for those beings who love her well.

Anyone who knows Mary as Mother and submits to her and obeys her in all things will soon grow very rich; every day, he or she will amass treasures, by the secret power of her philosopher's stone. "He who glorifies his Mother is like one who amasses treasure.". . . It is in the bosom of Mary that the young become old in light and holiness and experience and wisdom. . . .

Mary is the dawn that precedes and reveals the Sun of Justice. . . . The difference between the first and second coming of Jesus will be that the first was secret and hidden, the second will be glorious and dazzling; both will be perfect, because both will come through Mary. This is a great and holy mystery that no one can understand; "let all tongues here fall silent."

Louis-Marie Grignion de Montfort

"How," I asked Father Seraphim, "can I know that I am in the
grace of the Holy Spirit? I do not understand how I can be certain that I am in the Spirit of God. How can I discern for myself His true manifestation in me?"

Father Seraphim replied: "I have already told you, Your
Godliness, that it is very simple and I have related in detail how
people come to be in the Spirit of God and how we can recognize His presence in us. So what do you want, my son?"

"I want to understand it well," I said.

Then Father Seraphim took me very firmly by the shoulders
and said: "We are both in the Spirit of God now, my son. Why
don't you look at me?"

I replied: "I cannot look, Batiushka, because your eyes are
flashing like lightning. Your face has become brighter than the
sun, and my eyes ache with pain."

Father Seraphim said: "Don't be alarmed, Your Godliness!
Now you yourself have become as bright as I am. You are now
in the fullness of the Spirit of God yourself; otherwise you
would not be able to see me as I am." Then bending his head
toward me, he whispered softly in my ear: "Thank the Lord
God for His unutterable mercy to us! You saw that I did not
even cross myself; and only in my heart I prayed mentally to
the Lord and said within myself: 'Lord, grant him to see clearly
with his bodily eyes that descent of Thy Spirit which Thou
grantest to Thy servants when Thou art pleased to appear in
the light of Thy magnificent glory.' And you see my son, the
Lord instantly fulfilled the humble prayer of poor Seraphim.
How then shall we not thank Him for this unspeakable gift to
us both? Even to the greatest hermits, my son, the Lord God
does not always show His mercy in this way. This grace of
God, like a loving mother, has been pleased to comfort your
contrite heart at the intercession of the Mother of God herself.
But why, my son, do you not look me in the eyes? Just look,
and don't be afraid! The Lord is with us!"

After these words I glanced at his face and there came over
me an even greater reverent awe. Imagine in the center of the

sun, in the dazzling light of its midday rays, the face of a man talking to you. You see the movement of his lips and the changing expression of his eyes, you hear his voice, you feel someone holding your shoulders; yet you do not see his hands, you do not even see yourself or his figure, but only a blinding light spreading far around for several yards and illumining with its brilliance both the snow-blanket which covered the forest glade and the snowflakes which besprinkled me and the great elder. You can imagine the state I was in!

"How do you feel now?" Father Seraphim asked me.

"Extraordinarily well," I said.

"But in what way? How exactly do you feel well?"

I answered: "I feel such calmness and peace in my soul that no words can express it."

"This, Your Godliness," said Father Seraphim, "is that peace of which the Lord said to His disciples: 'My peace I give unto you: not as the world giveth, give I unto you' (John 14:27). What else do you feel?" Father Seraphim asked me.

"An extraordinary sweetness," I replied.

And he continued: "This is that sweetness of which it is said in Holy Scripture: 'They shall be drunken with the fatness of Thy house, and of the torrent of Thy delight shalt Thou make them to drink' (Ps. 36:8). And now this sweetness is flooding our hearts. . . . What else do you feel?"

"An extraordinary joy in all my heart."

And Father Seraphim continued: "When the Spirit of God comes down to man and overshadows him with the fullness of His inspiration, then the human soul overflows with unspeakable joy, for the Spirit of God fills with joy whatever He touches. You my son, have wept enough in your life on earth; yet see with what joy the Lord consoles you even in this life! What else do you feel, Your Godliness?"

I answered: "An extraordinary warmth."

"How can you feel warmth, my son? Look, we are sitting in the forest. It is winter out-of-doors, and snow is underfoot. There is more than an inch of snow on us, and the snowflakes are still falling. What warmth can there be?"

I answered: "Such as there is in a bathhouse when the water is poured on the stone and the steam rises in clouds."

"And the smell," he asked me, "is it like the smell of a bath-house?"

"No," I replied. "There is nothing on earth like this fra-grance. When in my dear mother's lifetime I was fond of danc-ing and used to go to balls and parties, my mother would sprinkle me with the scent which she bought at the best shops in Kazan. But those scents did not exhale such fragrance."

And Father Seraphim, smiling pleasantly, said: "I know it myself just as well as you do, my son, but I am asking you on purpose to see whether you feel it in the same way. It is ab-solutely true, Your Godliness! The sweetest earthly fragrance cannot be compared with the fragrance which we now feel, for we are now enveloped in the fragrance of the Holy Spirit of God. . . .

"Our present state is that of which the Apostle says: 'The Kingdom of God is not meat and drink; but righteousness, and peace in the Holy Spirit' (Rom. 14:17). Our faith consists not in the plausible words of earthly wisdom but in the demonstration of the Spirit and power (see 1 Cor. 2:4). That is just the state we are in now. Of this state the Lord said, 'There are some of them that stand here, which shall not taste of death, till they have seen the Kingdom of God come with power' (Mark 9:1). See, my son, what unspeakable joy the Lord God has now granted us!"

"I don't know Batiushka," I said, "whether the Lord will grant me to remember this mercy of God always as vividly and clearly as I feel it now."

"I think," Father Seraphim answered me, "that the Lord will help you to retain it in your memory forever, or His goodness would never have instantly bowed in this way to my humble prayer and so quickly anticipated the request of poor Seraphim; all the more so, because it is not given to you alone to under-stand it, but through you it is for the whole world, in order that you yourself may be confirmed in God's work and may be use-ful to others. The fact that I am a monk and you are a layman is utterly beside the point. What God requires is true faith in Himself and His only-begotten Son. In return for that the grace of the Holy Spirit is granted abundantly from on high. The Lord seeks a heart filled to overflowing with love for God and our neighbor; this is the throne on which He loves to sit and on which He appears in the fullness of His heavenly glory. Son, give me thine heart (Prov. 23:26; see Matt. 6:33), for in the human heart the Kingdom of God can be contained."

Motovilov

We all long for heaven where God is, but we have it in our power to be in heaven with Him at this very moment. But being happy with Him now means:

Loving as He loves,
Helping as He helps,
Giving as He gives,
Serving as He serves,
Rescuing as He rescues,
Being with Him twenty-four hours,
Touching Him in his distressing disguise.
Mother Teresa

THE NEW CREATION

This earth and all that is in it, and the whole cosmic order to which it belongs, has to undergo a transformation; it has to become a "new heaven and a new earth." Modern physics helps us to realize that this whole material universe is a vast "field of energies" which is in a continuous process of transformation. Matter is passing into life and life into consciousness, and we are waiting for the time when our present mode of consciousness will be transformed and we shall transcend the limits of space and time, and enter "the new creation."

There is a remarkable anticipation of this view in the Letter to the Romans, where St. Paul speaks of the whole creation "groaning in travail." For the creation, he says, "waits with eager longing for the revealing of the sons of God." The "revealing of the sons of God" is of course, the passage of humanity into the new state of consciousness. For "we ourselves," he says "groan inwardly as we wait for the adoption of sons, the redemption of our bodies." Our adoption as sons is our passing from human to divine consciousness, which is the destiny of all humanity. And this will come through "the redemption of our bodies." The new consciousness is not a bodiless state; it is the transformation of our present body consciousness, which is limited by time and space, into a state of transformed body consciousness which is that of resurrection. In the resurrection Jesus passed from our present state of material being and consciousness into the final state when matter itself, and with it the human body, passes into the state of the divine being and consciousness, which is the destiny of all humanity.

This is the "new creation" of which St. Paul speaks and which is revealed more explicitly in the Second Letter of Peter, where it is said, "According to his promise we await a new heaven and a new earth in which righteousness dwells." This is the ultimate goal of human history and of the created universe. . . . Our present world is conditioned by our present mode of consciousness; only when that consciousness passes from its present dualistic mode conditioned by time and space will the new creation appear, which is the eternal reality of which our world is a mirror.

Bede Griffiths, A New Vision of Reality

A COMMUNION OF PERSONS IN LOVE

I look out on this world of things around me, each one separated in space, each one moving in time, and beyond this comparatively stable world I know that there is an almost infinite dispersion of matter in space, a perpetual flux of movement in time. The one Word has gone out of itself, has reflected itself in this ocean of matter, the one Spirit is at work with its infinite energy, building up this matter in time. In my consciousness this diffusion of matter, this flux of becoming, begins to be ordered in space and time. But there is a window in my consciousness where I can look out on eternity, or rather where this eternal Reality looks out on the world of space and time through me. When I turn back beyond my senses and beyond my reason and pass through this door into eternal life, then I discover my true Self, then I begin to see the world as it really is. This is the archetypal world, not known in its diffusion in space and time, not reflected through a human consciousness dependent on a material body, but the world in its eternal reality, gathered into the one consciousness of the Word. Here all is one, united in a simple vision of being. All the long evolution of matter and life and man, all my own history from the first moment that I became a living cell, all the stages of my consciousness and that of all human beings, is here recapitulated, brought to a point, and I know myself as the Self of all, the one Word eternally spoken in time.

But does this mean that here all differences and distinctions disappear? Does this mean that I am God? Here I must remember that what I am trying to describe is a mystical reality, which cannot properly be expressed in human terms. I am straining human speech in order to try to bring it within the grasp of my mind. If I am using the ordinary language of rational thought, then certainly I am not God, and to say that this world is God is as false as to say that it exists of itself. If I try to find words to express that transcendent Reality, I have to use images and metaphors, which help to turn my mind toward the truth, and allow Truth itself to enlighten it. I can say that that eternal world is like the white light of the sun, in which all the colors of the rainbow are present and in which each retains its own distinctive character. Or I can say that it is like a symphony in which all the notes are heard in a single perfect harmony, but in which each has its own particular time and place. Or I can say that it is like a multitude of thoughts gathered together in a single mind which comprehends them in a single idea embracing all. Or going deeper, I can say that it is like a communion of persons in love, in which each understands the other and is one with the other. "I in them and thou in me, that they may become perfectly one." This is as far as human words can go.

Bede Griffiths, Return to the Center

Notes

Voices of the First World

p. 2 The Yokuts are a Native American tribe of California.

p. 3 The Maori are a Polynesian people native to New Zealand.

p. 6 The Kagaba are a tribe of Brazil, South America.

p. 6 Nut was the ancient Egyptian goddess of the sky, mother of the sun, moon, and stars, often called "She who bore the gods."

p. 6, second selection: Leon Shenandoah is chief of the Onondaga (1990).

p. 7 In this chant, the Navaho word *hozhoni* expresses the qualities of beauty, peace, and harmony.

p. 8, first selection: Black Elk was a nineteenth-century chief of the Oglala Sioux.

p. 8, second selection: From an 1851 speech by the Duwamish-Suquamish chief Sealth (Seattle).

p. 9, second selection: From a speech by Smohalla of the Nez Perce Indians perhaps from around 1850.

p. 11 Enheduanna (ca. 2300 B.C.) is the earliest identified author of either sex in world literature. She was the daughter of the Sumerian King Sargon, and a high priestess in the cult of the moon goddess Inanna.

p. 13 This account of the myth is from the Kiowa people, New Mexico.

Taoism: The Way of the Tao

pp. 19–26 Lao Tzu (b. ca. 571 B.C.), perhaps a legendary figure, was a Chinese Taoist mystic master. Modern scholars believe the *Tao Te Ching* was written by several people and did not come into its present form until the second half of the third century. Its ideas, however, show real cohesion, so a guiding figure might have been present in its compiling.

pp. 18, 27–30 Chuang Tzu (ca. 369–286 B.C.) was a leading Taoist mystic and cosmic comedian. Using parable and anecdote, allegory and paradox, he set out the early ideas of what was later to become the Taoist school.

p. 31 *I Ching*, "The Book of Changes," is an ancient Chinese book of oracles deeply inspired by Taoism. One of the sacred mystical masterpieces of humanity, *I Ching* has been revered for nearly three thousand years in

China and now enjoys great respect in the West; it is currently studied by psychologists and scientists as well as seekers.

p. 32 Liu I Ming (b. 1737) was a Taoist adept and a scholar of Buddhism and Confucianism. "The Height of Heaven, the Thickness of Earth" is taken from his *Awakening to the Tao*, written in 1816 when Liu I Ming was almost eighty years old.

p. 33 Born in China's Hubei province in the early 1870s, Loy Ching Yuen became one of the best-known Taoist masters of his time, with a large following in Shanghai province.

Hinduism: The Way of Presence

The scriptures that form the basis of Hindu mysticism are considered to be directly inspired by God. In China, scriptures are often ascribed to a particular person to give them authenticity; in India, God is thought of as their author and the sages who "received" them are considered of little importance.

pp. 36–42 The Upanishads are the wellspring of India's greatest spiritual philosophies. Said to be about three thousand years old, they are the earliest living record of what Aldous Huxley called the "perennial philosophy": the certainty, born out of direct personal experience, that there is a spark of Godhead in every creature, and that to realize this is the goal of every human life. Etymologically, the word "Upanishad" suggests "sitting down near," that is, at the feet of an illumined adept in an intimate session of spiritual instruction. No one knows exactly when these great texts were composed or who composed them; modern scholars agree that they were probably compiled about 800 B.C. Traditional Indian scholars date them ca. 1300 B.C.

pp. 43–46 The *Bhagavad Gita* (ca. fifth–second centuries B.C.) is the central text of the Hindu religion. It forms part of the great Indian epic *Mahabharata* and tradition claims that it was composed by Vyasa through direct divine inspiration. The sublime insights of the Upanishads are distilled in the *Gita* and made active in, and applicable to, ordinary life. In these excerpts, the god Krishna speaks to Prince Arjuna on the eve of the battle of Kurukshetra, urging him to go into action and teaching him the secrets of how to become "a humble instrument of my work."

p. 46 Kabir (1440–1518) is the best loved of all Indian mystic poets, revered by Hindus and Muslims alike. "Kabir" means "Great One" in Arabic. Kabir was an illiterate weaver in Benares; his songs were transmitted orally and continue to be sung all over India.

p. 47 Mirabai (ca. 1498–1546) is India's most famous woman saint. She was a Rajput princess who, when her husband—the crown prince of Mewar—died, refused to burn herself on his funeral pyre. She became a passionate devotee of Krishna and spent her last years as a wandering ascetic. Her songs, like Kabir's, are still sung all over India.

pp. 47–48 Mahadeviyakka, the Emily Dickinson of medieval India, lived in the twelfth century in South India and worshiped the divine as Shiva, god of creation and destruction. She is said to have been a naked wanderer, covered only by her hair. According to legend, she died into union with Shiva in her mid-twenties.

pp. 48–50 Ramprasad, a Bengali mystic of the eighteenth century, was a devotee of the divine Mother, whom he hymns with intensity and intimacy. He was the favorite poet of the great Hindu spiritual pioneer Ramakrishna. Although Ramprasad wrote hymns to several aspects of the divine Mother, most of his work is dedicated to the Mother as Kali—the "black" Mother of creation and destruction.

pp. 50–52 Jnaneshwar (1271–1293), called the "King of Saints," lived only twenty-two years, but he was one of the greatest mystics of India and wrote a highly regarded commentary on the *Bhagavad Gita* in Marathi. "The Nectar of Self-Awareness" is one of the supreme (though little-known) masterpieces of world mystical literature. Jnaneshwar, with dramatic wit and mystic subtlety, portrays the universe as the constantly changing "child" of the sacred marriage between Shiva and Shakti, the masculine and feminine creative powers. His vision of sacred balance, of there being "no God without a Goddess" and "no Goddess without a God," is a badly needed corrective to both "patriarchal" and exaggeratedly "matriarchal" understandings of the divine. What is especially moving in Jnaneshwar's vision is his awareness that the fundamental relationship between Shiva and Shakti is one of abandoned love, and not any kind of struggle for power.

pp. 52–58 Ramakrishna (1836–1886) was the most important, moving, and original of all modern Hindu saints. Born in Kamarpukur, a small village in Bengal, he lived most of his life in a temple (in Dakshineswar) near Calcutta. He proclaimed the oneness of all religions and mystical paths and gave a very comprehensive teaching, based on his own vast inner experience, on the mercy and divine power of the Mother. Modern mystics of the Mother consider Ramakrishna their most luminous and prophetic guide into her.

pp. 58–66 Aurobindo (1872–1950) was the greatest of all modern Hindu mystical philosophers and one of the pioneer spiritual intellects of humankind. Educated at Cambridge, where he was a brilliant classics scholar, Aurobindo refused a career in the civil service and returned to India to become an extremist nationalist. He was jailed, escaped to Pondicherry in French India, and spent the rest of his life there pursuing and articulating his vision of what he called "integral yoga." In his many mystic masterpieces, of which *The Life Divine* is the most important, Aurobindo fuse a Western vision of evolution, progress, and respect for matter with an Eastern understanding of the soul and the transforming Shakti ("force") of the Mother. If Ramakrishna is the "heart" of the modern "revolution of the sacred feminine," Aurobindo is its spiritual "mind." His is the mystic intelligence that has described most exhaustively and "scientifically" what it is like to be transformed by the Mother, "the conscious force that upholds us and the universe."

Buddhism: The Way of Clarity

pp. 71–75 The Buddha, known as Shakyamuni Buddha, lived between ca. 563 and 483 B.C. Born as a prince of the Shakyas in a tiny kingdom at the foot of the Himalayas, Shakyamuni as a young man enjoyed every pleasure that money and power could buy. One day he went beyond the walls of his palace and was devastated by what he saw: death, sickness, the anguish and suffering of the world. He then set out on a passionate search to find the way to end suffering which culminated in his enlightenment under the famous Bodhi-tree in Bodhgaya seven years later. After over forty years of wandering and teaching all over northern India, he left his body in his eighties. The *Dhammapada*—a collection of short and pungent verses ascribed to the Buddha—is regarded by every school of Buddhism as an authentic mystical masterpiece.

p. 74 The "Doctrine of Dependent Origination," developed here by the Buddha with his customary relentless precision, is one of the most important perceptions ever given humankind and the clearest description in any mystical tradition of the way in which "interdependence" of all phenomena exists and works. Modern ecologists and systems theorists as well as contemplatives derive great guidance and inspiration from this doctrine, and it also forms the analytic "basis" of later "descriptions" of "emptiness" and the inherently "void" nature of all phenomena.

p. 76 The *Questions of King Milinda* is a collection of pithy and brilliant "dialogues" concerning the basic tenets of Buddhism between King Milinda and the sage Nagasena; it was composed probably in the second century B.C.

p. 78 The *Prajnaparamita* texts are considered the originating texts of the Mahayana, the universal, "messianic" vehicle of Buddhism. Western and Buddhist scholars agree that they began to emerge into prominence in India from about 100 B.C., about four hundred years after the Parinirvana (Final Nirvana) of the Buddha in ca. 483 B.C. Western scholars believe they were created by leading Indian Buddhist mystics of that era but attributed to Shakyamuni Buddha as deriving from his direct mystical inspiration. Traditional Mahayana Buddhist scholars believe the sutras actually record the teaching of the Buddha, though these texts were spirited away from the human realm by gods and dragons only after four centuries. The texts of the *Prajnaparamita* had a boundless influence not only on the North Indian Mahayana schools (whole curricula were built around their study and contemplation) and so on the Tibetan and Mongolian monastic schools, but also on the Ch'an and Zen traditions.

p. 79 A bodhisattva is a being who renounces Nirvana to help all sentient beings attain liberation. The idea of the bodhisattva is the supreme contribution of Mahayana Buddhism to the world's mystical imagination.

p. 80 Nothing concrete is known about the "original text" of the sutra bearing Vimalakirti's name; it claims to record events that took place during the Buddha's historical lifetime (ca. 563–483 B.C.), but no text became current in India until Nagarjuna's time (first century B.C.–first century A.D.). It was subsequently translated into all the major "Mahayana" languages and became one of the most beloved of all philosophical texts.

p. 82 Shantideva was a monk who lived in the great North Indian Buddhist university of Nalanda in the early eighth century. He was a follower of Mahayana Buddhism, a school that emphasizes the pursuit of enlightenment for the benefit of all sentient beings, and not simply for the individual's sake. His masterpiece, the *Bodhicharyavatara*, roughly translated as "Entering the Path of Enlightenment," is especially beloved by Tibetan Buddhists.

p. 83 The thirteenth Dalai Lama (Buddhist god-king and spiritual leader) of Tibet is Tenzin Gyatso (1935–). Nagarjuna is widely considered the most brilliant of all the early Mahayana philosophers. Scholars are not yet completely agreed as to when he lived, but the evidence points to between the first century B.C. and the first century A.D.

p. 84 Paltrul Rinpoche was a nineteenth-century Tibetan Buddhist master.

p. 84 Saraha was a Buddhist monk-poet who lived in the ninth century.

p. 85 Seng Ts'an (d. ca. 606) was a Chinese Zen master, the Third Founding Teacher of Zen.

p. 86 Huang Po (d. ca. 850), also known as Hsi Yun, is regarded as the founder of the Lin Chi sect. He lived below Vulture Peak on Mount Huang Po, in the district of Hao An. His teachings blaze with iconoclastic rigor.

p. 87 Shutaku (1308–1388) was a Japanese Zen monk of the Rinzai school. His poem "Mind Set Free in the Dharma-Realm" is considered by Japanese Buddhists to be among the finest in their language, an astonishingly precise as well as moving account of enlightened consciousness.

Judaism: The Way of Holiness

All the translations from the Bible are from the Authorized Version of 1611, except the excerpts from the "Song of Songs." More "scholarly" translations have been done since; but the poetic splendor of the King James Bible has never been matched.

p. 91 Genesis, the first book of the Bible, opens with the Hebrew word *bereshit*, which means "in the beginning." The word *genesis*, "origin" in Greek, was later used as the title of the book because of its concern with the "origin" of the world and of the human race.

pp. 92–95 The book of Psalms (eighth–third century B.C.), the most familiar and widely used book of the Bible, is a collection of sacred songs. The one hundred and fifty psalms in the book of Psalms portray all the various moods of the Jewish mystic relationship with God—awe at his power and magnificence, gratitude for his mercy, fear at his judgment, tender rapture at his grace. The author is unknown but is traditionally said to be King David.

pp. 95–97 "Song of Songs" means the "greatest of songs" and according to Jewish commentaries portrays, in exquisite poetic form, the mutual love of God and his people. The book may have been compiled from different marriage hymns, and its sensuousness has made it a favorite text of both Jewish and Christian mystics. Although the Song of Songs is attributed to Solomon in the traditional title (Song of Solomon), the language and style of the work point to its being written in a time after the end of the exile in Babylon (ca. 538 B.C). In Christian tradition the Song of Songs is interpreted in terms of the mystical union that exists between Christ and the church and, by Bernard of Clairvaux particularly, in terms of the "marriage" between Christ and the individual soul.

pp. 97–98 Isaiah was the greatest of the Hebrew prophets who lived in the eighth century B.C. The vision of the Messiah on p. 98 comes from the latter part of the book of Isaiah, sometimes called the Deutero-Isaiah, and is generally ascribed to an anonymous poet who prophesied toward the end of the Babylonian exile.

p. 99 The book of Daniel takes its name not from its author, who is unknown, but from its hero. Daniel was a young Jew taken early to Babylon, where he survived until at least 538 B.C. Strictly speaking, this book does not belong to the prophetic writings but to a distinctive type of literature known as "apocalyptic." The book of Daniel was composed during the terrible persecution carried on by Antiochus IV Epiphanes (167–164 B.C.) and was designed to comfort the Jewish people in their ordeal. The "fourth" that "walked with" the men in the furnace was seen as a "sign" of the messiah.

p. 100 The book of Sirach derives its name from the author, Jesus son of Eleazar, son of Sirach. Its earliest title seems to have been "Wisdom of the son of Sirach." We know little about the author except that he was a sage, lived in Jerusalem, and probably wrote his book between 200 and 175 B.C. in Hebrew. In the book of Sirach, wisdom (Hebrew *hokmah*) is hymned as "feminine" in poetry of great majesty and passion. Later on, this understanding of Hokmah as "feminine" would be expanded into the kabbalistic vision of the Shekinah (from the Hebrew meaning "to dwell"): the fundamentally transcendent vision of Hokmah in Sirach becomes more immanent and the Shekinah, the "bride" of Yahweh, is now seen as dwelling in and permeating creation. As Anne Baring and Jules Cashford remark in *The Myth of the Goddess* (London: Viking, Arkana, 1991), p. 470: "Where are we to trace the origin of this idea if not to the goddess who was once Queen of Heaven and Earth and united in her person those dimensions that (later), in Judaism, were separated in the name of Yahweh?"

p. 101 The book of Wisdom was written ca. 100 B.C. Its unknown author was a member of the Jewish community in Alexandria, Egypt. He wrote in Greek, in a style patterned on that of Hebrew poetry. The power of the "sacred feminine" aspect of God has rarely been expressed more precisely or nobly.

pp. 101–104 *Pirke Avot* is a collection of rabbinic sayings compiled sometime between 250 and 275, although most of the sages quoted in the text lived far earlier. The names of the early rabbis have been preserved in the text itself. Very little is known about them individually, but, taken together, they speak in one great, sane voice of the necessity of enacting holiness and making prayer real in service of others and the world, of letting go of the illusion of fragmentation and bringing things into harmony with each other.

pp. 104–111 These texts are taken from Daniel C. Matt's magnificent *The Essential Kabbalah* (HarperSanFrancisco, 1995), a crucial work for the understanding of Jewish mysticism. "The Chain of Being" was written by Moses de León (thirteenth century). "Ein Sof and You" is by Moses Cardovero (sixteenth century). "In the Beginning" comes from the *Zohar* (thirteenth century). "Water, Light, and Colors" was written by Moses Cardovero. "The Journey of the Soul" is by Moses de León. "The Song of Songs" was written by Abraham Isaac Kook (twentieth century). "Sexual Holiness" has been translated by Daniel Matt from an anonymous book, the thirteenth-century *Iggeret ha-Qodesh*.

The Hebrew word *kabbalah* means "receiving" or "that which has been received." In kabbalistic mysticism, which began in the twelfth century, the aim of mystical discipline was to effect the marriage of the Shekinah (divine immanence) with her "partner," the Holy One. For those Jewish mystics, God was conceived not as static being but as dynamic becoming. Without conscious human participation, they believed, something in the essential nature of God remains unrealizable. As Daniel Matt puts it: "It is up to us to realize the divine potential in the world. God needs us." As any reading of these sublime texts makes clear, the kabbalistic mystics were original and radical pioneers of a holistic vision that united "heaven" with "earth" and "body" with "soul," and their attempts seem especially relevant today. Although all of these texts were written by men in a very "masculine" tradition, their embrace of *this* world and *this* body and of the dynamic nature of the partnership between God and human beings makes them exciting to modern feminist mystics and mystics of the Mother.

p. 111 "The Glorious End of Rabbi Shimon" is taken from "The Wedding Celebration" in the *Zohar*, the central Jewish mystical text (*zohar* means radiance, so the title translates as "The Book of Radiance"), written by Moses de León in thirteenth-century Spain. Rabbi Shimon was said to be a famous teacher of the second century who lived in Israel and spent twelve years in a cave. This passage begins with Rabbi Shimon speaking.

Ancient Greece: The Way of Beauty

p. 116 Gaia was the ancient Greek goddess of the earth. One of her most important shrines has been uncovered at Delphi. The name "Gaia" is now heard everywhere; in the "Gaia hypothesis" of physicist James Lovelock, which maintains that the planet earth is one completely self-regulating system; in "gaia consciousness," which urges that the earth and her creatures be thought of as one interdependent unity; and simply in the term "gaia," which expresses a deep reverence for the planet as a being who is alive and on whom all life is dependent. As Anne Baring and Jules Cashford comment in their book *The Myth of the Goddess*: "Underlying this phenomenon is the idea that only a personification of the earth can restore a sacred identity to it, or rather, her, so that a new relationship might become possible between humans and the nature world we take for granted" (p. 304).

p. 117 I felt it essential to include in this anthology as detailed and clear an account as possible of the Eleusinian mysteries, because of their enormous secret influence on the Greek mind. Plato, for instance, may have been initiated into them as a young man; the experience, if legend is accurate, transformed him into a philosophic mystic. Also, the mysteries were essentially Mother-mysteries, as this account shows, mysteries of the understanding of the sacred feminine. In the years to come when the spiritual world will see a great flowering of creativity in the re-creation of ancient rituals, the Eleusinian mysteries will have a lot to suggest and contribute.

The purpose and essential meaning of the mysteries was initiation into a vision. "Eleusis" means "the place of happy arrival" (this is where "Elysian fields" comes from). The term "mysteries" comes from the word *muein,* which means to close eyes and mouth, and indicates the veil of secrecy that was kept drawn over the ceremonies.

We can see from the account of the mysteries included here that two essential features of religious ceremony, possibly dating from Neolithic times, are present also at Eleusis—the sacred marriage and the birth of the divine child. This imagery—of the sacred marriage between opposites, between heaven and earth, body and soul, masculine and feminine, heart and mind, and the birth from that marriage of a new kind of human being, the divine child—is central to all mystic understanding of the work of the sacred feminine and is echoed in suggestive ways in the deepest insights of all the mystical traditions.

pp. 118–119 Heraclitus lived and flourished about 500 B.C. The greatest of all the pre-Socratic Greek philosophers, he belonged to an eminent family and his thought and writings were famous for their difficulty. Heraclitus was nicknamed "the Obscure" and "the Riddler" but, in fact, his cryptic apothegms yield their astonishing secrets to sustained meditation and reveal a spiritual intellect of the deepest richness and brilliance. Heraclitus's "fragments" survive embedded in later texts, of which Hippolytus's *Refutation of All Heresies* is the most important. Born in Rome, Hippolytus (180–235) was a Christian and a fierce controversialist; he was chosen as "antipope" and exiled to Sardinia. His *Refutation of All Heresies* in ten books contains much information about "pagan" philosophy. I have retained his comments about Heraclitus because they are singularly clear and respectful.

p. 121 Empedocles (ca. 495–435 B.C.) came from Acragas in Sicily from a rich and distinguished family. He wrote several works, all of them in verse, of which only portions of "On Nature" and "Purification" remain.

The long fragment I have chosen to excerpt here comes from a text by Simplicius in which it was embedded—his commentary on Aristotle's *Physics*. Simplicius flourished about 500–540 in Alexandria. Empedocles' great poem shows an astonishing understanding of the interplay of "opposites" within the whole—an understanding worthy of the Taoist and Hindu mystics and presented with an entirely original subtlety and drama.

pp. 121–132 Plato lived from ca. 428 to 348 B.C. His family was an ancient one with political connections in high places; he had a wide acquaintance with the prominent men of his time, traveled extensively abroad, and at the age of forty founded the Academy and directed its affairs until his death. Plato's influence on all subsequent philosophy cannot be exaggerated; what is too little appreciated is the mystical depth of his thought and its surprisingly intense and forthright visionary quality. Because of the vast influence of his theory of ideas, which suggests essentially that all visible "created" things are more or less faulty simulations of perfect ideas, another, more positive side of his vision, one that sees the world as permeated with "soul" and as a "blessed god," has not received comparable attention. Both sides of his vision of reality are celebrated here.

Socrates was Plato's "master," his spiritual hero, and the "mouthpiece" through which he expressed many of his major ideas. Ironic, brilliant, and uncompromising, Socrates infuriated the respectable and was put to death, after a rigged trial, by being forced to drink hemlock. Plato was probably in his mid-twenties when Socrates was executed.

pp. 132–137 Plotinus (204–270) has been called the last great philosopher of antiquity, although in more than one respect he was a precursor of modern times. The *Enneads*—his mystic masterpiece—brings together Platonism, mystic passion, and ideas from Greek philosophy as well as striking variants of the Trinity and other crucial Christian doctrines to produce an original synthesis. What I have tried to show in my selection of his work is that, despite his tendency to "transcendentalize" (and with what high passion!), Plotinus was also—as a true mystical "lover" of reality—overwhelmed by the beauty of *this* world that he, like Plato, saw as "saturated" with "soul."

p. 138 Marcus Aurelius (121–180) was the most famous of the Stoic philosophers. Stoicism began around 310 B.C. and derives its name from *stoa,* meaning "porch," the place in Athens where Zeno, its founder, pronounced his discourses. Stoics saw God as the living universe and as its supreme ordering Intelligence; a spark of this divine truth was, they believed, in everyone. Although the Stoics insisted that there was only One Power, they knew it to have many aspects and referred to each by a different name—Providence, Law, Destiny, Nature, etc.

Marcus Aurelius was the last of the great Roman emperors. This excerpt is from the small journal he kept toward the end of his life, which was later to be known as the *Meditations* and to become one of the world's best loved books. What Marcus Aurelius's style combines are two usually incompatible things—real exaltation of mind with great humility and directness.

Islam: The Way of Passion

pp. 141–144 The Qur'an is universally known as the sacred book of Islam. The name *qur'an* means "recital" or "reading." According to its own claims, the Qur'an is a revealed book in the tradition of the Torah of Moses and completes earlier messages from the divine to humanity.

The Qur'an was revealed through the Prophet Muhammad, who was born ca. 570. Muhammad came from the noble Quraish clan, the custodians of the sacred shrine of Mecca. He was orphaned at an early age, but grew into a responsible young man. At twenty-five he married his employer, Khadijah, a successful businesswoman. The first divine revelation came to Muhammad when he was forty years old and took place during one of his occasional retreats in a mountain cave outside Mecca. Muhammad was far from "inflated" by the experience; it was so shattering that he was scared and deeply, reverently shaken. Revelation after revelation followed, Muhammad was hailed as a prophet by followers, and Islam began to spread, often against fierce opposition. Forced to flee from Mecca in 622, the Prophet reentered it in triumph eight years later. He cleared its sacred shrine of idols and established worship of the one real God, Allah. Through the promulgation of the Qur'an and his own example as a noble and inspired prophet, Muhammad also reformed many aspects of family, social, and economic life.

It is impossible to exaggerate the sacred importance to Muslims of the Qur'an. To "ordinary" believers it offers infallible truths and guidelines; to the mystic, it is a document with numerous levels of transmission, each one of which has a meaning in accordance with the understanding of the reader.

In my selection I have concentrated on those passages from the Qur'an that tended to be most loved and discussed by the later Islamic mystics, passages in which the glory of Muhammad's all-embracing vision of God's majesty are most beautifully enshrined.

p. 145 The *Hadiths* are the "prophetic sayings" of Muhammad. These are not in the Qur'an but are considered canonical. Many of them were preserved by the Prophet's wife, Aisha, and they give a glimpse into the depths of Muhammad's fiery and profound mystical intellect. They are of crucial importance to the development of Islamic mysticism; most of its insights, perceptions, and stances can be traced to their bold formulations of the mysterious love of God and its transformatory power.

p. 146 Al-Hallaj (ca. 858–922) was one of the founders of Sufi mysticism and its supreme example of surrender and sacrifice. He was hung, drawn, and quartered in the main square of Baghdad for proclaiming *An'al Haqq*, "I am the Supreme Reality."

p. 146 The greatest woman Sufi mystic poet, Rabi'a (717–801) was born— the fourth daughter of a poor family—in Basra, in what is now Iraq. She was orphaned young and sold into slavery. Later she was freed by her master when he recognized the depths of her spiritual understanding and lived for most of the rest of her life in a retreat house on the outskirts of Basra. Many people came to study with her. She was famous for her simple way of life and for the depth of her surrender to God.

pp. 147–150 Ibn Arabi (1165–1240) was born in Myrcia, Spain, became a Sufi at twenty, and after a lifetime of travel and teaching settled in Damascus in 1223, where he died. The greatest of all Sufi philosophers, he was also a considerable poet. This should not surprise us in a writer who said of himself: "In what I have written I have never had a set purpose, as other writers. . . . Flashes of divine inspiration used to come upon me and overwhelm me. . . . Some works I wrote at the command of God, sent to me in sleep or through mystical revelation."

pp. 150-155 Farid Ud-din Attar was born during the twelfth century at Nishapur in northeast Iran. His date of birth is given by different scholars at various times between 1120 and 1157; the earlier date is likely. After wandering all over the Middle East and Asia in search of spiritual instruction, he returned and settled in his hometown, where he kept a pharmacy and wrote his masterpiece, *The Conference of the Birds*. He died ca. 1220.

pp. 156-165 The greatest of all Sufi mystical poets, Rumi is considered by many to be the greatest mystical poet of humankind. Born in 1207 in Balkh, Afghanistan, Rumi died in Konya, southern Turkey, on December 17, 1273. The first part of Rumi's life was spent as a brilliant scholar and theologian. Then, in December 1244, he met the man who was to transform him—a wandering dervish called Shams I Tabriz. Rumi's son Sultan Valad wrote of this meeting, "After meeting Shams, my father danced all day and sang all night. He had been a scholar—he became a poet; he had been an ascetic—he became drunk with love."

Shams disappeared—probably murdered—two years later, but the terrible grief that seized Rumi only drew him deeper into the mysteries of divine love. He survived the death of his beloved to devote the rest of his work to the glory of his memory and to the transmission of the vision that their love had given him.

pp. 166-167 Mahmud Shabestari (ca. 1250–1320) is named after his birthplace—Shabstar—which is in Iran near Tabriz. He spent most of his short life there and died there. *The Rosegarden of Mystery* is his most famous work and considered one of the masterpieces of Persian mystical literature. Lahiji's commentary on it is also revered. Lahiji was born in Lahijan, near the Caspian Sea, and died in Shirz in 1507. His commentary not only illuminates Shabestari's words with marvelous clarity but also contains superb descriptions of his own mystical experiences.

pp. 167-169 Kaygusuz Abdul was a Turkish Sufi who died in 1444. The text of the original can be found in Nuruous Maniye Library, Istanbul.

Christianity: The Way of Love in Action

pp. 173-181 Jesus Christ (3-36) who lived, taught, and died in Palestine (what is now Israel), was the founder of Christianity. Christ's supreme and challenging originality lay in the combination in his teaching of the highest mystical awareness with the most simple and egalitarian vision of service and action. It is this fusion, at every level of inward prayer and external action, of an understanding of the laws of "Heaven" with their enactment on earth that makes Christ the son of the Mother as well as the Father and his teaching the most potent example we have of the sacred marriage between the "transcendent" and "immanent" knowledge of God.

pp. 181-183 The *Gospel of Thomas* was discovered by Professor Gilles Quimpel in Cairo in 1956. Scholars now accept that this Gospel transmits the original Aramaic sayings of Jesus that were preserved by members of his brother James's group in Jerusalem and that it was one of the earliest sources drawn on for the sayings in the Gospels of Matthew and Luke. The Gospel of Thomas opens with the words "These are the secret words which the Living Jesus spoke and Didymos Judas Thomas wrote. And He said, 'Whoever finds the explanation of these words will not taste death.'" If the mystic Christ that we meet so vividly in this Gospel had been the Christ who most influenced the growth and development of Christianity, the history of Western civilization would have been different.

pp. 183-187 As a youth, Paul (3-64), who was then called Saul, was a brilliant and fierce opponent of Christianity. A vision on the road to Damascus convinced him, however, that Jesus was the Messiah. The next thirty years of his life were spent traveling, teaching, and bringing together the many new Christian groups. Through his leadership and the extraordinary example of his courage and spiritual depth, the different precepts of the new faith were welded into a universal religion of redemption.

A careful reading of Paul reveals him as a very advanced mystic who perfected a balance between contemplation and action. What is remarkable in Paul's vision and prophetic of the development of Christian mysticism is his profound humility before the mystery of God. Paul never claimed to be "enlightened" or "achieved"; the nakedness of his self-honesty set the tone for all future Christian mystics.

p. 187 The desert fathers, so called, were a group of intrepid and absolutist hermits who retired in the fourth and fifth centuries to the deserts of the Near East to seek solitude and contemplation. Their sayings, handed down orally, were collected in the *Verba Seniorum*. Thomas Merton writes of them, "The Desert Fathers declined to be ruled by men, but had no desire to rule over others themselves. Nor did they fly from human fellowship. The society they sought was one where all men were truly equal, where the only authority under God was the charismatic authority of wisdom, experience and love" (*The Wisdom of the Desert: U.S.A.* [New Directions, 1970], p. 5).

pp. 188-190 Gregory of Nyssa (ca. 330–94) was the greatest of all the early Christian mystics after the apostle Paul. Born in Cappadocia, in his early life he was influenced by the pagan ideals of the emperor Julian and became a teacher of rhetoric. Later he became Christian and rose to become bishop of Nyssa and a close advisor to the emperor Theodosius. Gregory's "doctrine" of "epectasis," the "doctrine of infinite growth," is one of the most important and radical developed by a mystic of any tradition. Gregory's vision of an endless evolution in God corresponds to the visions of Rumi and Aurobindo. It is radical because it undercuts all pretensions to "static" enlightenment. As Gregory reminds us "the path that lies beyond our immediate grasp is infinite."

p. 190 There are few figures in the history of Western spirituality more enigmatic than the fifth- or sixth-century writer known as Pseudo-Dionysius, or Dionysius the Areopagite. His real identity is unknown and even the exact dates of his writing have never been determined. Yet his influence and the influence of his negative "apophatic" philosophy, which stresses the rapt impotence of the human mind before God, were widespread. The way of Dionysius was a way of self-emptying, and many of the greatest later mystics were very marked by his work. Modern historians of religion have noted the similarities between Dionysius's position and that of *jnana yoga* in Hinduism, and the Madhyamika school of dialectics in Mahayana Buddhism founded by Nagarajuna.

p. 191 Augustine (354–430), bishop, philosopher, and Doctor of the church whose thought molded the Western theological tradition, is one of the most powerful figures in the history of the church. His *Confessions* reveal both the struggle and the deep visionary experience that permeated his philosophical and theological speculations.

pp. 191–192 The "Akathistos Hymn," still sung in the Eastern Orthodox Church, was written by Romanus the Melodist, a Greek Byzantine monk, in the fifth century. I have included it here not only for its beauty but also because it shows the glory accorded to Mary in the early church. Although Mary plays only a very small role in the Gospels, early movements in the Christian church increasingly brought out her role and her power, until in 431 at the Council of Ephesus Mary was proclaimed not only "Christbearer" but also "God-bearer" (Theotokos). Although the new titles accorded Mary stopped short of proclaiming her the divine Mother, it is clear from this hymn by Romanus that all the powers and beauties of the Mother of antiquity were constellated around her. Mary is, in fact, the unrecognized mother goddess of the Christian tradition. The complete recognition of this is now taking place among modern mystics and feminist theologians, and Christianity is being revealed as a "double yoga" of Mother and Child, Jesus and Mary. Jesus' teaching is coming to be seen as a "voicing" of the silence of his Mother, as radical a teaching of the "sacred feminine" as has ever been given humankind.

p. 192 Symeon the New Theologian (940–1022), Greek Orthodox abbot, poet, and theologian, was born in northern Turkey in Paphlagonia. In 1001 he was banished for his controversial views to a small town on the Asiatic shore of the Bosphorus, where he spent the rest of his life.

pp. 192–194 Meister Eckhart (1260–1329) was perhaps the most influential Christian figure of the Middle Ages. His ideas and writings—highly controversial in their time (and officially condemned by the Catholic church)—were not only embraced by the great Christian mystics, such as Teresa of Avila and John of the Cross, but also represent the beginnings of German philosophy and mysticism.

p. 194 An extraordinary polymath whose work is being increasingly studied and celebrated, especially by feminist mystics and theologians, Hildegard of Bingen (1098–1179) was a German abbess, healer, visionary, painter, composer, preacher, and fierce social critic.

pp. 194–196 Francis of Assisi (1182–1226) is perhaps the best loved of all Christian saints. A great mystic whose passion for Christ led him to bear his stigmata, Francis founded the Franciscan order, which is dedicated to living in the holy poverty of the early Christians. Francis's love for all creation—his biographer tells us that even worms "kindled within him infinite love"—inspires any who allow themselves to encounter it.

pp. 196–197 A great, tormented Franciscan mystical poet, Jacopone da Todi (ca. 1230–1306) was one of the first to write not in Latin but in the vernacular. He entered the (Franciscan) Order of Friars Minor during the last quarter of the thirteenth century. His "Lauds" contain some of the greatest poems in the Christian mystical tradition.

pp. 197–198 Juliana of Norwich (1342–1416), an English recluse, experienced healing after visions of Christ and the Virgin Mary. Her *Revelations of Divine Love* is one of the loveliest of all mystic texts and her vision of Christ the Mother is becoming increasingly influential.

pp. 198–199 Bernard of Clairvaux (1090–1153) was a great Cistercian mystic and pioneer of Marian devotion. His *Four Homilies in Praise of the Virgin Mary*—from which this excerpt is taken—are perhaps the most comprehensive mystical celebrations of the force of the sacred feminine ever written in the Western tradition.

p. 199 Mechthild of Magdeburg (ca. 1207–1282 or 1297) was born into a wealthy German family. In her first vision, at age twelve, she saw "all things in God, and God in all things." In 1235, she joined a community of Beguines, independent groups of laywomen dedicated to leading a life of charity, poverty, chastity, and spiritual practice. In 1270 she entered the convent of Helfta, where she died.

pp. 199–200 Biographical information about Hadewijch of Antwerp is scant, but we know that she was a Flemish Beguine who lived in the thirteenth century and in her later life headed a small group of contemplatives. She has recently been rediscovered as the most important exponent of love mysticism and one of the major figures in the Western spiritual tradition.

p. 200 Angela of Foligno (1248–1309) was a married woman whose husband and children died shortly after her heart had been mystically opened to Christ. The atmosphere where she lived in Foligno (in Umbria) was fresh with the memory and presence of Francis of Assisi. Angela's "revelations" of her mystic experiences as related in her *Memorial* and *Instructions* are extreme, volcanic, and unmistakably authentic.

pp. 201–204 John Ruusbroec (1293–1381), for many the greatest of all the Christian mystics and one of the central mystics of humankind, lived as a monk in the duchy of Brabant and spent the later part of his life in a hermitage in the forest of Groenendaal near Brussels. Anyone who reads him will discover in his work a mind of the rarest power, capable of describing with exquisite precision the highest mystical states. His work is especially important for its understanding of the necessity for marrying contemplation and action: the human being who wants to live the full and fully mature mystical life has, Ruusbroec claims, to marry within himself or herself the two aspects of the nature of God—God's "fecundity" and God's "tranquillity in repose"—to go toward God in "external work" and live in God "by his fruitive inclination in eternal rest."

pp. 204–207 Born in Fontiveros, John of the Cross (1542–1591) was the son of an impoverished weaver. He became a Carmelite friar in 1563 and in 1564 went to the University of Salamanca for four years. The decisive meeting of his life was with Teresa of Avila, who asked him for his help in her mission to reform the Carmelite order. After terrible sufferings at the hand of the Inquisition, John died in Ubeda in 1591, leaving behind him a body of work in both prose and poetry unmatched in Christian mystical literature for its analytical brilliance, honesty, and depth of spiritual passion. His poems are considered to be among the greatest in Spanish.

pp. 207–208 Teresa of Avila (1515–1582) was born into a noble Spanish family, one of a dozen children. She embraced the cloister in 1536 and for the next twenty years underwent a severe spiritual journey which led in 1555 to a desire to create with the new Discalced Carmelites a return to holy poverty. The rest of her life was occupied in this movement of reform. Called a saint even in her own lifetime, Teresa was nevertheless a most practical, funny, and loving human being, tirelessly active as well as ecstatic. One of her favorite remarks was, "The Lord lives among pots and pans." For Teresa, as for Ruusbroec, "Martha and Mary must combine"; the full mystical life is one of prayer *and* service.

p. 209 Thomas Traherne (1637–1674) was an English priest and ecstatic mystic poet. The anonymous manuscripts of his *Poetical Works* and *Centuries of Meditation* were found in a London bookshop in 1895. Edited by Bertram Dobell, the poems were published in 1903, and the *Centuries* in 1908 to immense acclaim. In Traherne, we have one of the most sustainedly joyful of all mystics, one who worshiped *this* world as the site of a perpetually unfolding theophany of divine beauty and "felicity."

pp. 210–211 Angelus Silesius is the pseudonym of Johannes Scheffler (1624–1677), born to Protestant parents in the Silesian capital of Breslau seven years after the Thirty Years War had begun to tear Europe apart. At the age of twenty-nine, after graduating from the University of Padua, he converted to Catholicism and took the name Angelus. Although he pursued a career as a fierce apologist, it is the depth of his mystical epigrams that have secured his place in any history of Christian mystical thought.

pp. 211–212 Louis-Marie Grignion de Montfort (1673–1716) was, after Bernard of Clairvaux, the most inspired of all Marian visionaries. Montfort's exploration of the mystical "link" between the "return" of Mary and the "second coming" of Christ is being increasingly seen as one of the greatest spiritual adventures in Christian mystical thought and highly relevant to modern times. Born in Brittany, Montfort became a priest early and founded the Missionaries of the Company of Mary, known as "Montfortians," and the Daughters of Wisdom. He was canonized in 1947.

pp. 213–216 Seraphim of Sarov (1759–1833), a contemporary of Pushkin, was a great Russian saint. He became a novice at nineteen, and at twenty-eight took his monastic vows and received the name of Seraphim. His sanctity and simplicity made him famous all over Russia. He was the model for Father Zossima in Dostoyevsky's *The Brothers Karamazov.* Motovilov was Seraphim's disciple. He was miraculously cured of paralysis by the saint. This "holy conversation" took place during the winter of 1831 in the heart of the forest near Sarov.

p. 216 Mother Teresa is a modern-day saint who lives and works among the "poorest of the poor" in Calcutta, India.

pp. 216–218 Bede Griffiths (1906–1993), born into the English middle class, was educated at Oxford. He entered the Catholic church and became a Benedictine in the early 1930s. After twenty years as a Benedictine monk and scholar, he went to India, where he lived the last four decades of his life, working on a profound synthesis between Eastern and Christian mysticism and living the completely simple life of a Hindu *sannyasin.*

꒐

Selected Bibliography

Aurobindo. *Letters on Yoga*. Three volumes. Pondicherry, India: Sri Aurobindo Ashram, Publication Department, 1971.

———. *The Mother*. Pondicherry, India: Sri Aurobindo Ashram, Publication Department, 1972.

Baring, Anne, with Jules Cashford. *The Myth of the Goddess: Evolution of an Image*. New York: Viking Press, 1991.

Boff, Leonardo (translated by Robert Bar and John W. Doercksmeier). *The Maternal Face of God: The Feminine and Its Religious Expressions*. New York: Harper & Row, 1977.

Eliade, Mircea. *From Primitives to Zen: A Thematic Sourcebook of the History of Religions*. New York: Harper & Row, 1977.

Easwaran, Eknath. *The Bhagavad Gita*. Tomales, CA: Nilgiri Press, 1985.

Griffiths, Bede. *Return to the Center*. Springfield, IL: Templegate, 1977.

———. A New Vision of Reality. London: HarperCollins, 1989.

Fox, Matthew. *The Coming of the Cosmic Christ*. San Francisco: HarperCollins, 1980.

Harvey, Andrew. *The Way of Passion: A Celebration of Rumi*. Berkeley, CA: Frog, Ltd., 1994.

———. *The Return of the Mother*. Berkeley, CA: Frog, Ltd., 1995.

Hixon, Lex. *Coming Home: The Experience of Enlightenment in Sacred Traditions*. Burdett, NY: Larson Publications, 1995.

Lawlor, Robert. *Voices of the First Day: Awakening in the Aboriginal Dreamtime*. Rochester, VT: Inner Traditions International Ltd., 1991.

Ramakrishna. *The Gospel of Ramakrishna*. Translated into English with an introduction by Swami Nikhilananda. Mylapore, Madras, India: Sri Ramakrishnam Math. N.D.

Shaw, Miranda. *Passionate Enlightenment: Women in Tantric Buddhism*. Princeton, NJ: Princeton University Press, 1994.

Smith, Huston. *The World's Religions*. San Francisco: HarperCollins, 1991.

Tarnas, Richard. *The Passion of the Western Mind*. New York: Harmony Books, 1991.

Underhill, Evelyn. Mysticism. Notre Dame, IN: One World Publications, 1993.

Watts, Alan. *The Wisdom of Insecurity: A Message for an Age of Anxiety*. New York: Vintage Books, 1980.

Wilber, Ken. *Eye to Eye: The Quest for the New Paradigm*. New York: Anchor Books, 1983.

———. *Sex, Ecology, Spirituality*. Boston: Shambhala Publications, 1995.

———. *A Brief History of Everything*. Boston: Shambhala Publications, 1996.

◯

Grateful acknowledgment is made for permission to reprint excerpts from the following works: Selections from the Upanishads and the Bhagavad Gita reprinted by permission from *God Makes the Rivers to Flow* by Eknath Easwaran, copyright © 1991, Nilgiri Press, Tomales, CA. *Return to the Center* by Bede Griffiths, by permission of Templegate Publishers. *A New Vision of Reality* by Bede Griffiths, HarperCollins Publishers, Ltd. Bernard of Clairvaux, Homily 2 on *Missus est*, translated from the Latin by Marie-Bernard Said OSB, in *Bernard of Clairvaux: Homilies in Praise of the Blessed Virgin Mary*, Kalamazoo, Michigan: Cistercian Publications, pp. 30–31, copyright © Cistercian Publications, 1979. From *A Wonderful Revelation to the World by Saint Serapohim* translated by Archimadrite Lazarus Moore, first published in the *Orthodox Life* vol. 4, 1953, with a revised edition by Nectarios Press, Seattle, WA, 1993. From Sermon Nineteen of Meister Eckhart; *Sermons and Treatises* vol. I by M.O.C. Walshe copyright © M.O.C. Walshe 1979 from Element Books Ltd. of Shaftesbury, Dorset. Selections from *The Mother*, the *Life Divine*, and *Savitri* by Sri Aurobindo from the Aurobindo Ashram Trust, Pondicherry, South India. A translation of Rumi, "Borrow the Beloved's Eyes," by Coleman Barks in *We Are Three* from Maypop Books, Athens, GA, 1987. Thich Nhat Hanh's translation of the *Heart Sutra*, reprinted from the *Heart of Understanding: Commentaries on the Prajnaparamita Heart Sutra* by by Thich Nhat Hanh, 1988, with the permission of Parallax Press, Berkeley, CA. Two translations of Ramprasad from *Mother of the Universe* by Lex Hixon, reprinted by permission from Quest Books, Theosophical Publishing House, Wheaton, IL. "Hymn to Gaia" and "Eleusinian Mysteries: To Die Is to Be Initiated" from *The Myth of the Goddess* by Anne Baring and Jules Cashford (1991) with the permission of the authors and Arkana Books Ltd. Excerpts from *The World's Wisdom: Sacred Texts of the World's Religions* by Philip Novak, copyright © 1994, reprinted by permission of HarperCollins *Publishers*, Inc.

Five prayer hymns from *Women In Praise of the Sacred* by Jane Hirshfield, copyright © 1994 by Jane Hirshfield, reprinted by permission of HarperCollins *Publishers*, Inc. Excerpts from *The Essential Tao*, translated and presented by Thomas Cleary, copyright © 1991 by Thomas Cleary, reprinted by permission of HarperCollins *Publishers*, Inc. Excerpts from *The Essential Koran*, by Thomas Cleary, copyright © 1994 by Thomas Cleary, reprinted by permission of HarperCollins *Publishers*, Inc. Excerpts from *The Essential Kabbalah* by Daniel C. Matt, copyright © 1995 by Daniel C. Matt, reprinted by permission of HarperCollins *Publishers*, Inc. "Truth" and "Ojibway Prayer" from *The Sacred Ifa Oracle* by Afolabi A. Epega and Philip John Neimark, copyright © 1995 by Afolabi A. Epega and Philip John Neimark, reprinted by permission of HarperCollins *Publishers*, Inc. "Bride," "Dark Night," and "The Fountain" translated by Willis Barnstone from *St. John of the Cross*, copyright © 1972 by Willis Barnstone, reprinted by permission of New Directions Publishing. Selections from the Dalai Lama from *Essential Teachings* by the Dalai Lama, by permission of North Atlantic Books, copyright © 1995 North Atlantic Books. All Biblical excerpts in the Judaism and Christianity sections are taken from the 1611 King James Version, unless otherwise indicated in the Notes. The following selections appear in original translations by the editor, Andrew Harvey: in the section on Islamic mystics, the Hadiths, the first two poems by Rabia, all of the Rumi poems except "Borrow the Beloved's Eyes," as noted above, Lahiji's commentary on Shabestari; in the Christian section, the *Hymn to the Sun* by St. Francis, the fifteen epigrams by Angelus Silesius, the excerpt from Louis-Marie Grignion de Montfort.